Here's what people are saying about this book:

"Mack and Sara do a great job of walking you through the process of publishing in an easy to understand format."
—**John Kremer**, *1001 Ways to Market Your Own Book*

"Sara and Mack do a fantastic job with their book. Their advice and support are what helped me bring my goals to reality. I highly recommend this book to any writer seeking expert advice, motivation, and encouragement."
—**Dr. Joye M. Carter,** *My Strength Comes from Within*

"Many people offer advice on how to get published. But this book is unique because it offers both information and inspiration between the covers of one book."
—**William July II,** *Understanding the Tin Man & Brothers, Lust & Lies*

"*How to Self-Publish & Market Your Own Book* is an easy to comprehend, step-by-step guide for all aspiring writers. It is a must for those seeking a clear and concise understanding of commercial literature."
—**Troy Martin**, *Dazed & Confused-Surviving Life in the Game*

"The information you provided was accurate, useful, simple and effective. I used other resources on my journey to becoming published but your book was the road map. It was one of my best investments."
—**Jetola Anderson-Blair,** *In My Sister's Shoes*

"Mack and Sara have broken down an often intimidating process into simple terms with sample forms, practical examples, and money-saving tips, not to mention invaluable Internet and other great resources. I highly recommend this book!"
—**Tia Shabazz,** Founder & Executive Director, Black Writers Alliance

How To Self-Publish & Market Your Own Book

A Simple Guide for Aspiring Writers

How To Self-Publish & Market Your Own Book

A Simple Guide for Aspiring Writers

Mack E. Smith
Sara Freeman Smith

U R Gems™

GROUP

How To Self-Publish & Market Your Own Book
A Simple Guide For Aspiring Writers

By Mack E. Smith & Sara Freeman Smith

Copyright © 1998, 2001 by Mack E. Smith & Sara Freeman Smith
Revised Second Edition

Publisher's Cataloging-in-Publication
(Provided by Quality Books, Inc.)

Smith, Mack E.
  How to self-publish and market your own book : a simple guide for aspiring writers / Mack E. Smith, Sara Freeman Smith.
  -- 2nd ed.
  p. cm.
  How to self-publish and market your own book
  Includes bibliographical references (p.) and index.
  LCCN 99-090415
  ISBN 0-9662328-7-9

  1. Self-publishing--United States. 2. Books--United States--Marketing. I. Smith, Sara Freeman. II. Title. III. Title : How to self-publish and market your own book.

Z285.5.S65 2001   070.5'93'0973
                         QB100-901570

Printed in the United States of America.
Printed on acid free paper.

Published by: U R Gems Group, Inc., Houston, TX

This publication is designed to provide accurate and authoritative information with regard to the subject matter covered. It is sold with the understanding that the publisher is not engaged in rendering legal, accounting or other professional advice. If legal advice or other professional assistance is required, the services of a competent professional person should be sought.

[From the "Declaration of Principals" jointly adopted by a committee of the American Bar Association and a committee of Publishers and Associations.]

The Authors and U R Gems Group, Inc., individually or corporately, do not accept any responsibility for any liabilities resulting from the actions of any parties involved.

Table of Contents

CHAPTER 10   137
New Tools for the Millennium
Alternative publishing options: E-books, print-on-demand, e-zines

CHAPTER 11   151
Dynamic Literary Organizations
Publishing, writing, reading organizations that support authors

Foreword

When I finished my first book, I decided to self-publish it because I realized no publisher would be interested in a technical book on the parachute. Although no traditional publisher picked up my book, it was an instant success. My experience was not unique. Every year, hundreds of thousands of manuscripts are rejected by publishing houses. Most of these manuscripts are never read unless an agent presents it to a publisher. Many talented authors believe their work was rejected because it was simply not good enough to be printed. Authors who have successfully self-published their books know better.

These are exciting times for authors. Increasing opportunities are being made possible by personal computers, electronic publishing, print-on-demand, and the Internet. The initial investment costs to self-publish and market books have declined significantly. Other obstacles such as book returns, inventory storage, and book damages are declining because of new technology. New rules are being adopted as new alternative publishing options emerge. Authors can now choose several ways to produce their works.

Mack and Sara use their personal experiences to simplify the process of publishing and marketing your own book. They not only provide easy-to-understand guidelines, they also motivate aspiring writers to overcome obstacles on their journey to a successful publication. And they do it well.

Dan Poynter, *The Self-Publishing Manual*

http://ParaPublishing.com

Other Books by the Authors

Turning Stones Into Gems

An Inspirational Self-Development System
(Sara Freeman Smith)

Turning Stones Into Gems
A Prayer & Gratitude Journal
(Sara Freeman Smith)

How to Self-Publish & Market Your Own Book
Workbook

About the Authors

Mack and Sara have self-published nine books and reports since 1997. They have helped numerous authors and entrepreneurs publish their own fiction, non-fiction, and poetry books. They are cofounders of U R Gems Group, Inc., a publishing and consulting firm with headquarters in Houston, Texas. Their firm provides seminars, workshops, teleclasses, personal coaching, book marketing, and book coordination services for aspiring writers and self-publishers. Mack and Sara conduct workshops and speak at conferences across the country. They developed a web site, www.writershelpdesk.com, which offers valuable resources and inspiration for emerging writers.

Acknowledgments

We give praise and glory to God for blessing us with the desire and ability to help others achieve their dream of writing a book.

Our love and thanks to our son, Rashod for his understanding and valuable help with our book's revision. You are an amazing man-child!

Thanks to our wonderfully talented cover designer, Gladys Ramirez.

Thanks to our editors, Sonya Vann, Rae Baskins, and Tina Dickerson, your suggestions were terrific.

To each of you that contributed to our book with advice, resources and words of encouragement, a million thanks!

To Dan Poynter and John Kremer, you both are simply the best!

A special thanks goes to the Association of Authors and Publishers, especially Rita Mills. With your help, we started our publishing business on a sound foundation.

An extra special thanks to the following people for all your advice, support, and referrals: Rikki Mayer-Franklin, Larry Hayes, Alethea Nelson, Chikodoli Lott, Phyliss R. Dixon, Sam Uzoh, Lisa Whitlock, Kandi Eastman, Brian Egeston, Herb Metoyer, Daryl Green and Sara's *bestest* friend, Gwen Richie.

Thanks to every aspiring writer who encouraged us to write this book and used our advice to become published authors.

Thank you for reading our book. We pray for success in your publishing endeavors when you succeed, we succeed.

INTRODUCTION

Congratulations! You have just made an important step on the road to publishing your own book. You made a decision to write a book and you took action by purchasing a resource book to help answer your questions. *How to Self-Publish & Market Your Own Book* was written to help you solve a problem and assist in your research while you pursue your dream of writing a book.

We all know people who decide to start an endeavor, they dream about it, think about it, and talk about it but they never actually do it. They never take action. We commend you for taking action and wish you great success on your journey to publishing your own book.

Timing is an important factor in the success of any endeavor and it's not an accident that you are writing a book at this time in your life. The timing is right and the time is now! You have a message that should be told. In recent years, the publishing industry has experienced significant changes and innovations that make the time right for aspiring writers. Major improvements in technology allow printers to have a book to a consumer in less than fifteen minutes or you could read a Stephen King novella from your computer monitor or download, print and read it later. E-publishing or electronic publishing (e-books) will become increasingly more prevalent in the future and will be discussed in detail in Chapter 10. Yes, all these innovations are viable and available alternatives for publishing your book. *How to Self-Publish & Market Your Own Book* offers the tools, tips, and resources to help you publish and market your book.

Who Should Benefit From This Book?

Aspiring writers, new authors, and beginning publishers will refer to *How to Self-Publish & Market Your Own Book* as a useful resource. Oftentimes, women and minorities face special challenges when trying to get published due to traditional values held within the publishing industry. These challenges include limited or unknown resources, and misconceptions regarding buying trends, target audiences, and affordable publishing options. *How to Self-Publish & Market Your Own Book* will dispel those misconceptions to ensure that women and minority writers have the same opportunity for success in their writing endeavors as any other writers.

Perhaps you have already finished your manuscript and were turned down by agents and publishers. Have you begun to doubt you have what it takes to become a successful author? Did you know that publishers rejected *Chicken Soup for the Soul* 33 times? Well, it's true. Nevertheless, the authors never gave up believing in their message and neither should you. A Florida publisher, Health Communications, finally bought their manuscript and the rest is history! The *Chicken Soup for the Soul* series is a publishing phenomenon!

You may be a new author with a book requiring a boost in its marketing efforts to increase your sales. A new book will usually garner a six-month publicity campaign from a publisher. As the author, you must continue to keep your book in front of the public. *How To Self-Publish & Market Your Own Book* offers new creative methods to help you reach your target audience and market your book.

Hard Cold Facts

This book reveals some of the cold, hard facts about writing and publishing a book. You definitely must devote a lot of time and energy to the project without any guarantees. The commitment you will need on the road to publishing and marketing your own book is enormous. You must have a *passion* for your work. This passion serves as a vehicle to keep you on the road to success. Expect many obstacles along the way, but keep your passion alive. If you do not maintain your enthusiasm, others will recognize this and may not buy into your cause. Let's face it, if you are not excited about your book, why should anyone *else* be excited?

Good News for Self-Publishers

The publishing industry is changing rapidly, especially for writers interested in self-publishing. Did you know that one of the longest running best-selling business books, *Who Moved My Cheese?* was initially self-published by Spencer Johnson? Even best-selling author Stephen King embarked on the self-publishing route in the summer of 2000. Without the assistance of his publisher, King offered to write a new novel (*The Plant*) online by having readers buy a chapter a month. Many in the publishing industry predicted that his project would fail but it was successful. In the first week, more than 150,000 people downloaded the first chapter and more than 76 percent of them paid a dollar! At that time, King committed himself to writing a chapter each month if his readers would support him through the honor system by paying a dollar to read a chapter.

More people are deciding to self-publish and are ultimately being picked up by major chains. Technology is making it easier to publish and market books in less time than ever before. Additionally, you do not have to rely on bookstores alone to sell your book. You can now use the Internet, hand-held devices (pocket readers), the gigantic mail-order industry, catalogs, libraries, toll-free numbers, e-mail, organizations, and non-traditional markets to sell your book. *How to Self-Publish And Market Your Own Book* explores these options throughout the book.

Remember, a great dream is merely a dream until you ***make*** it a reality.

Chapter 1

Before You Spend Your Time

and Money...

"Don't spend a thousand dollar's worth of time on a quarter's worth of results"

Before you consume precious time writing your manuscript or spend valuable money on your book, it's time for a reality check. Writing is an art. *Publishing is a business.* For many people, writing a book is also a business. Writing a manuscript can be considered the first step in starting a business venture. Before you start this business, first ask yourself the following questions:

Why do I want to write a book?
The reason you write a book should complement the reader's need to be informed, inspired, or entertained. If your book does not meet those needs, you will have difficulty selling your book.

Do I want to self-publish or get published? Why?
You must decide how much control and involvement you want with your book's production. Each option carries distinct requirements and you must be comfortable with your choice.

Do I understand the advantages and disadvantages of both?
You must thoroughly understand the advantages and disadvantages unique to each option *How to Self-Publish & Market Your Own Book* will help you make an informed decision regarding your choice.

Do I know how my book will be sold?
You have to realize that books can be sold to your audience other than through the traditional bookstore, friends and family network or word of mouth. You must learn how to think out of the box and explore different methods to sell your book outside your comfort zone or traditional means.

Do I expect to earn a profit once my books are sold?
Believe it or not, some people publish books just for the fun of it and making money is not important. On the other hand, most of us would like to make money while having fun. If you expect to make money with your book, you need a plan of action. *How to Self-Publish & Market Your Own Book* will provide a plan or strategy for your book to earn a profit.

Do I have a passion for my work? Can others feel my passion?
If you have an insatiable desire to publish your book after all the discouraging comments from friends, family, peers or national publishing firms, that's your passion! You take every opportunity to tell others about your desire to publish and they can sense your passion.

Can I wear the many hats of a literary entrepreneur?
You must be very versatile as an entrepreneur. You will be a sales rep, an accountant, a publicist, inventory analyst, a banker, a speaker, and a writer to name a few! If you can only handle one or two of these tasks, then decide if you can find others to help you.

Can I engage others to wear certain hats, i.e., editor, graphic designer, printer, marketer/publicist, distributor, attorney, accountant, business manager, etc.?
You will have to develop contacts through networking with the publishing and writing community to handle those projects that you cannot perform.

Can I write what I know? Do I know how to write it?
Don't try to write about something with which you are unfamiliar. Rely on subject matter that you are qualified to write about in your book. You may need to enroll in some writing courses offered by your local university, community college, personal learning centers or online to enhance your writing skills.

Do I know who will buy my book and why? How do I get my book to them?
You must identify who will want to buy your book and the methods you will use to get your book to them.

Are there other books already published on my subject? Can I make mine unique?
You can research your subject by finding similar books at your bookstore or online bookstores. Try to determine what differentiates your book from your competition.

Am I willing to spend years promoting my book?
Writing your book is a major commitment that will require more than a few months' or even years' endeavor. The genre

or subject of your book and its timeliness will determine how long you can promote and market your book.

Am I willing to learn as much as possible about the publishing industry?

You will need to join and participate in publishing events sponsored locally, regionally, or nationally. You can ask authors, inquire at bookstores, or search the Internet for writing and publishing organizations and events.

Can I set clear goals and follow a plan?

You must have a goal or vision regarding your book. Once you have a goal, develop your plan to get you there. Marketing plans are discussed in detail in Chapter 8.

If you are unsure about some of your answers to these questions, you should carefully consider your book project. Your answers to these questions are vital to your success in publishing your book. If any of your answers are unfavorable, begin to think about ways to overcome those challenges before you venture further with your book.

The following questions will require serious thinking. These answers will help you develop a marketing plan and you should write down your answers for reference.

What is your subject or genre?

A genre is the category or specific area(s) your book will fit. Your book may qualify for one area or several, such as fiction - romance, sci-fi, mystery, or nonfiction - self-help, reference, inspirational, etc.

Once you determine the genre of your book, you will be better equipped to research similar books, get ideas for the title of your book, etc.

What is your book about?
You should write a one-minute commercial about your book. If you can say what your book is about in 30-45 seconds, use the remaining seconds to tell the potential customer why he or she will benefit from buying your book.

What will your book consist of?
You will determine if your book will have an introduction, index, reference section, glossary, charts, graphs, photos, maps, illustrations, graphics, etc.

What other books would you consider your competition? What makes your book different?
Know your competition! Do your research to gather information. Begin your research at your local library, bookstore or online. Look in *Books in Print* (www.bowker.com) for books similar to your book. Find out how many books are published with subject matter similar to your own. If there are a large number of books just like yours, you need to try to differentiate or separate your book from the competition. Always focus on what will make someone buy your book over your competition.

You can also search on the Internet and online bookstores to compare prices and check the number of pages for each book. You can use this data to help price your book competitively. Chapter 3 explains pricing in more detail.

When do you want to see your book finished?
Your answer will depend on how much time and money you want to invest in your project. Using offset printing, you can have a completed perfect bound book from a printer in two to three months once you finish your manuscript (proofed and edited). However, new technology has paved the future for alternative publishing options that allow a book to be available in 30 days or less. (See Chapter 10).

Think about a reasonable time frame in which to complete your book and develop a time line to achieve it (we discuss production time lines in the Appendix). Determine how much money you will need to achieve your goal. Will you be able to pay this amount? How will you finance your book project, i.e., bank loan, credit card, family loan, savings, etc?

How will you fill your orders for your books?
Filling and shipping your orders can be very time consuming if your book is successful. If you, your family, or friends fill the orders, what happens when you are out of town conducting book events, speaking engagements, etc.? Will your orders go unfilled for several days or weeks? Can you afford to have a customer wait that long for your book? If you take orders for your book, don't forget you need a toll-free number. A toll-free number enables you to take orders around the country. Some people will not place an order unless you provide a toll-free number. You can contact any major telephone communications company for information.

You have another option using fulfillment companies that fill and ship orders for a fee. You must decide if this is a job you will want to do or whether to hire a firm to do it. A list of fulfillment firms can be found in our Resource Guide and in *Literary Market Place* under "Shipping Services" in your local library or online at www.literarymarketplace.com

These questions should start you thinking seriously about why you want to have your own book published. Perhaps you want to leave a legacy for your family. If this is your purpose, making a profit may not be important to you. However, if you want to change careers, you should be very focused on profits. If you only want the prestige of calling yourself an author, be prepared to pay for your prestige. If you do not know the answers to these questions, keep reading. Then go to the recommended readings/bibliography at the end of this book. Many of these resources can be found in your local library or bookstore. You can visit our web site www.writershelpdesk.com for additional resources.

Remember, as an author and publisher, you can never learn too much about self-publishing. The more you know, the less likely it is that you will make costly mistakes. Do not be afraid to ask for help when you are not certain you are correct. One avoidable mistake can cost you more money than you can afford to lose.

Chapter 2

A Closer Look At The

Publishing Industry

"Gather all the facts before making an informed decision"

The major publishing houses are located in New York. They receive thousands of queries and manuscripts each month from hopeful authors. Small Presses and University Presses receive an enormous amount of queries and manuscripts. Estimates vary on the number of queries and manuscripts publishers receive yearly, but it is safe to say it is a six-figure amount. According to digital publisher Xlibris™, only 10% of the 500,000 manuscripts that are written every year are ever published. This small percentage includes books printed by small publishing firms and self-publishers as well. First time novelists have less than a 1% chance of getting published. Obviously, the odds are against a major publisher accepting your book.

The name of the publishing game is to pick books that will sell. Many times the major publishers will go with authors who have a proven track record or are a national celebrity. So, if you are John or Jane Doe, you have a problem because many publishers are unwilling to take a chance on an unproven, new author. Remember, *writing is an art and publishing is a business.* In many ways, publishing is similar to banking. Publishers do not have unlimited budgets, and they are in business to earn a profit. Therefore, they have to decide on *which* books will most likely earn them a profit. They probably won't choose you until you prove your book is already a success. This attitude is similar to the old image of banks that won't lend you money unless you can use your money as collateral. In other words, you don't get the loan until you show them you don't really need it. You must show how you will pay the loan back within a reasonable time. The same principle applies to publishers who give an author an advance. They expect to sell enough books to quickly earn a profit after recovering advances and other costs. Similarly, publishers want you to *show them the money* before they take a chance on you.

Many popular and famous authors had to start their writing careers as self-published authors before they were offered substantial contracts by major publishing firms. The large publishing houses once rejected many of these authors, but they believed in their messages or stories and did not quit!

William July II, author of *Understanding the Tin Man*, began his career by self-publishing his first book into a best-seller. His success captured the attention of a literary agent who helped him secure a major publishing contract! Doubleday subsequently published a revised and expanded edition of his first book, *Brothers, Lust and Love.*

We discuss other alternative publishing options available to writers in Chapter 10 - New Tools for the Millennium.

Advantages of Self-Publishing

There are many advantages to publishing your own book. Oftentimes, publishing yourself is the only option you may have. This can be a blessing in disguise.

Control

One of the greatest benefits of self-publishing is that you can maintain control of the book's production and how your book will be marketed. Once you sign a contract with a major publisher, you relinquish control of your book project. For some authors, this is perfectly fine. They do not want to deal with the details. However, if you want to have input into the cover design, editing, title, marketing plan, testimonials, etc., then you want to self-publish. Do you want to determine which cities you want to include in your publicity plan? A publisher may decide to go on a limited book tour to certain cities and bookstores that you know will not reach your target audience. Also, don't be surprised if part of your big deal includes the rights to your next two books, as well.

When you self-publish a book, you are the boss. You're the person in total control. This is a lifelong dream for many people. You have your own business, are excited about your work, and love what you are doing. Being in control obviously has its advantages.

Money

Let's not forget about the money. All things being equal, you can make more money by self-publishing your own book. How much do you think you would earn from a book that retails for $20.00? Most would guess a reasonable amount of at least half or $10.00. In reality, authors earn far less. Your royalties would normally range between $1.00 and $3.00! Who gets the rest of the money? Your publisher and agent, of course! Well, if you self-publish, all the profits are yours after subtracting the costs of producing your book.

In most cases, advances paid by publishers are going to be four- or five-figure amounts. Royalties paid after the publisher earns back its advance will normally range from 5%-15% of the retail or wholesale price of the book. The big name authors are getting the 15% or $3.00 per book! Simple math can show you that the chances of earning more than 15 percent by self-publishing are very good. An example of possible profits is shown in Chapter 3—Taking Care of Business.

Timing

It should be no surprise that self-publishing is a faster process than the traditional publishing route. Isn't this true about businesses in general? Large corporations have policies and procedures involving multiple departments and employees that take time. You only have yourself.

A local publisher once said it takes his company a minimum of nine months to publish a book *after* the manuscript is done. For some major publishing houses, don't be surprised if it takes more than a year before a book is printed and available for purchase. Don't get us wrong, a lot of planning should go into publishing. The point is, you can probably do many things yourself, use independent professionals for other services, and still produce the book faster than most publishing houses. New technology has enabled stories to go from manuscript to book form within 30 days! These technologies are discussed in Chapter 10—New Tools for the Millennium.

Taxes

There can also be tax advantages to publishing your own book. As mentioned earlier, publishing is a business and any business can have tax write-offs. Many of the expenses incurred during the process of producing and selling your books may be deducted in your income tax return. We recommend that you discuss this with your CPA, tax accountant or tax attorney. These professionals are licensed and qualified to give advice in this area.

Disadvantages of Self-Publishing

Lack of Knowledge and Inexperience

Major publishers have decades of experience publishing books. They have developed a process to successfully publish a variety of books. They have made mistakes and learned from them. This is not to say they do not still make mistakes. If a publisher has already rejected you, then you know by now that the publisher made a mistake. Unfortunately, they have already been through what you are just beginning to experience. Their expertise is an advantage over your inexperience. They have a large team of professionals with a vast collective experience in all aspects of publishing.

Limited Budget

You probably have a very limited budget. Most of your budget is probably earmarked for printing the book. Publishers have larger budgets and more resources to assist with book promotion, sales, distribution, etc. Due to limited sources of financing, many self-publishers fund their first books by using credit cards, family loans, and bank loans

Limited Distribution Outlets

The major publishing houses have few problems getting books into virtually every major bookstore in America. Self-publishers can expect to face some challenges in getting their books into major bookstores without national distribution in place. Most bookstores order the majority of their books through national wholesalers or distributors (see Chapters 3 & 7). Major publishers have established relationships with them. Such wholesalers and distributors must accept self-publishers. Many will require a marketing plan or strategy along with your book information before deciding to accept your book. If your marketing plan is not targeted and realistic or your book is poorly printed, they may decide not to *accept* you as a client.

Vanity Press/Subsidy Publishers

If you plan to publish for profit, be extra careful with this type of publisher. A vanity or subsidy publisher is a type of publisher that *charges* an author to publish their book. The author usually pays *all* the costs of publishing, not just the printing costs. Figure on paying much more for this service than you would by contacting a traditional publisher yourself. In return for you financing the book project, a vanity press publisher agrees to promote and distribute the books.

When an author pays them a substantial fee to publish their book, they are often printing unedited manuscripts. After all, they made their money from printing the book, not selling, and distributing it. Unfortunately, reports of numerous problems with some vanity publishers cause many sources in the industry not to conduct business with them. For example, the Library of Congress will normally not assign a catalog card number to a vanity publisher. Most book reviewers will often automatically toss any book from this type of publisher. In addition, in many cases you may not own the copyrights to the book, even though you wrote the book and paid the production costs.

How to Identify a Vanity Press / Publisher

Vanity publishers often run advertisements seeking manuscripts. The ads often start out saying "Manuscripts Wanted... or ...Book Manuscripts Invited." You are almost certain to get a letter with favorable reviews after you send your manuscript. This positive interest in your book can be very tempting if you have received numerous rejections from other publishers. However, remember *traditional publishers do not charge you to publish your book.* They accept the risks associated with investing in a book that does not sell enough copies to earn a profit. This is the reason it is so difficult to get your book picked up by a traditional publisher. *They* lose if your book does not sell. *You* lose if the vanity publisher is unsuccessful.

Unknown authors can usually expect traditional publishers to offer royalty payments of five to ten percent. Vanity presses may offer royalty payments of up to 40% of book sales. Expressed another way, they get 60% commission off the books *you* paid them to print. This high percentage should be another red flag that you are dealing with a vanity publisher.

Many bookstore chains have lists of vanity publishers and will not do business with them. Also, don't be surprised if many book reviewers, wholesalers, distributors, and libraries reject a book published by a vanity press.

If you are not publishing your book to earn a favorable profit, then this section may not be of interest to you. Some vanity publishers have been in business for 50 years or longer. They have their niches and traditional publishers and printers have their niches as well. For more information on vanity publishers, call *Writer's Digest* at (513) 531-2222 and ask for *Should You Pay to Have it Published*. The report currently costs $3.00 and supplies may be limited (www.writersdigest.com).

Now that electronic publishing has gained acceptance and popularity, we have started to see some companies refer to e-book publishers as vanity publishers. Although many of them charge small fees to convert books to electronic formats, we do not consider them the same as traditional vanity publishers. We have heard of cases where traditional vanity publishers have charged over $25,000 to print a few hundred copies of a book. E-book publishers' set-up fees are usually less than $1,000. Some companies do not charge set-up fees at all.

Some of the electronic publishing houses are wholly or partially owned by major, well-respected organizations, such as Barnes & Noble, Inc., Borders, and Random House Ventures, etc. These companies have invested hundreds of millions of dollars in other established companies to sell books for authors. Their profits are derived from books sales and not their set up fees. They lose money if they do not sell books. A traditional vanity publisher usually earns most of its profit when the books are printed before any book is sold.

As mentioned earlier, you should check out every company before you engage their services. However, we applaud e-publishers for the opportunities they are giving authors to publish their work free or for a reasonable fee. Although, there is some valid concern regarding editorial quality on some of the e-book web sites, we believe this will diminish as more emphasis is placed on editorial review in the future.

How to Investigate a Publisher or Printer

If you want to do business with a publisher or printer that you are not familiar with outside of the majors in the industry, contact your local Better Business Bureau. This organization keeps a record of complaints and lawsuits filed on various companies. Find out if there are any unresolved complaints and the details of complaints that were resolved. This is a good practice before you do business with any company. You can also contact the Federal Trade Commission, Washington, DC 20580 to request information regarding complaints filed against a company.

If you are a member of professional publishing or writing organizations, ask them to refer you a reputable printer. Ask other self-publishers about their printers too. If the printers are not actively involved either locally, regionally, or nationally in a publishing trade organization, that's a red flag. Visit some online discussion rooms and ask other authors about the company. You will be amazed by the information that is shared. You should ask for references and verify them. Those references would include several of their clients, a bank reference, any public endorsements, professional organization memberships, etc. Your bank's credit inquiry section may be able to run a credit check for you.

Also, find out how long they have been in business and at their current address. Caution is especially advised if they have only been in business or at their current address a short time.

If you want to self-publish your book with the intent to earn a reasonable profit, it is recommended that you deal with traditional printers or digital printers (print-on-demand). If you are uncomfortable with marketing and distributing your book, there are various resources such as book distributors, online book marketers, trade associations, etc. that can help your efforts. Most of the companies that we deal with have been in business at least five years. The Appendix lists printing companies, trade associations, book distributors, and other resources that will put you closer to your goal of publishing your manuscript. Additional resources can be found in *Literary Market Place* in your local library.

Inclusion in our list of organizations should not necessarily be considered an endorsement, but rather a starting point in the selection process. You should do your homework on these as well, but you are better off starting with a company that at least appears to be established. The point is, you should investigate *before* you invest your money!

Chapter 3

Taking Care Of Business

"If you don't have time to do it right, when will you have time to do it over?"

Remember, we stated earlier that you should consider your manuscript as the first project of your new business. Most business owners are in business to make a profit. Therefore, this chapter is devoted to helping you learn how to get started self-publishing with a profit in mind. The key to your success is constant learning. Never assume you have learned everything, because the industry is constantly changing.

We highly recommend that you join a publishing association and attend some of its events. Your membership will entitle you to a wealth of resources and informational workshops, conferences and discounts. We recommend two national associations listed in our resource section that caters to small publishers. Both organizations sponsor multiple events throughout the year to assist the small publisher. Their members, other seasoned authors/publishers, are eager to offer their support, inspiration and suggestions that can be invaluable to a novice. Ask your local bookstores or librarian about local publishing or writing organizations that may be active in your city.

Book Expo America (BEA) is a must for every small publisher. This major international publishing event spans three days during the first week of June every year. American Booksellers Association sponsors multiple workshops, networking, and social events. Every major publishing house and major bookstores attend the event to showcase their latest books. Anyone that's in the book business will attend.   Participants   include   literary   agents,   media executives/producers, book reviewers, printers, online publishers, distributors, publicists, and best-selling authors. Everyone is on the lookout for the next *Chicken Soup for the Soul* or *Harry Potter* writer. You will learn all the latest technology in the publishing industry and make important contacts for marketing your book. You can get tons of free books from major publishers to aid in your future research.

Attending the BEA 2000 in Chicago provided helpful information and contacts in developing our book. The small publishing associations actively participate in every BEA. Plan to attend the Publishers Marketing Association's University Conference held three days before the BEA. The PMA event will supply information about planning strategies and contacts before you get to the BEA conference. It's held in the same city and you can network with other small publishers. Visit the PMA web site for details (www.pma-online.org).

Price

Setting a price for your book is very serious. This is one of the most important decisions you will make regarding your book. The price of your book should *not* be determined simply by what you want to earn from each book. The price your audience will pay for your book is *more* important. Always remember a customer will only buy if your book has a perceived value in comparison to similar books. If you are planning to sell to the high-end professional market (attorneys or physicians), you could set a price of $50.00 or more for your book. If your book retailed for less than $20.00, the perceived value could be questionable because comparable books are priced higher. However, if your audience is a low- or fixed-income group, don't expect them to pay $50.00.

The industry standard regarding pricing for offset printed books is between *five to eight times* the production costs of your book. We recommend you target at least *eight* times. The increasing popularity of electronic publishing is causing the publishing industry to reassess pricing such books, because these new forms are significantly less expensive to produce than traditional or offset printed books. Since e-books books are relatively new, you may not find a uniform standard of pricing. E-books are normally priced much lower than offset or print on demand books. However, their lower price is logical, because unlike traditional books, they cost substantially less to produce. Printed books can be sold for 50 - 65% less than their normal retail price in e-book format. For example, a paperback book that retails for $20.00 can sell from $7.00 to $10.00 as an e-book, depending on the genre and information contained in it.

You can compare prices of books similar to your own as a guideline to setting the price of your book, regardless of the format in which the book is published. Electronic publishing is discussed in more detail in Chapter 10. (See Chapter 10 for the list of resources of e-book publishers).You must always consider the price of other books on your subject before making a final decision. If possible, we suggest you test different prices for your book (see testing details in Chapter 7 - Promoting & Marketing Your Book).

Price your book competitively with books of similar size, page length and production quality. *Books in Print* is a good resource to assist you with this effort. Your local library should have a copy of this reference in book form or on computer disks. You should find a book in the same subject area as yours. For example, if you are writing a book on parenting, go to that subject in *Books in Print*. A similar book will have the same type of cover (hard, soft, full color), a similar number of pages, the same type of binding (perfect bound, hardback or spiral), and the same interior text (black, photographs, color graphics). Your book price should be the same as or comparable to the other books. However, sometimes it may advantageous to set your price lower or higher. For example, if you have the only book written on a topic especially for physicians, you may be able to justify a higher price. The best price can be determined by testing different prices and markets. However, testing is not always practical, particularly if your subject is very time sensitive.

Consider when pricing your book how you will sell your book: direct to the public or through various channels of distribution. Some distribution methods are more profitable than others. For example, if you plan to sell your book through mail order, you can normally expect to profit more per book than if you use a distributor. A book distributor will keep 65%-70% of the retail price of your book. If you are handling all the mail orders, you keep 100% of the price. Of course, there are expenses associated with mail order, but you should be able to hold them well below 65%-70% of the price of your book.

Other ways to market your book are through wholesalers, sales representative, online, seminars, book signings, specialty shops, corporations, bookstores, and libraries. We will also cover some of these methods in Chapter 7.

Cost

Once you have a price in mind for your book, you need to know how much your book will cost. A common rule of thumb is your cost should be one-eighth of the price of your book. Put another way, the target price of your book is eight times the production cost of your book. Remember, these are only guidelines.

Every method of formatting and selling your book will have different production costs associated with it. Consider all formats for your book such as offset printing, e-book, print-on-demand, CD-ROM, and audio book. Select the method(s) best for your book and your target market. Carefully review Chapter 10, New Tools for the Millennium, which discusses e-books and print-on-demand in detail.

The size of your book is another major factor that affects the cost of production. Books can have numerous shapes and sizes. Remember, the more creative and unusual the shape of your book, the more costly it will be to print. Libraries and bookstores have shelves with standard measurements to stack books for display. It's important that your book will fit the shelf if you want your book there. The most common and economical book size is 8 ½ x 5 ½, other popular sizes are 4 x 7 (also called mass market), 6 x 9, 7 x 9, 8 ½ x11, 4x 6 and gift books as small as 2x2! These sizes are acceptable for paperback and hardbound books. Carefully examine each method you are considering for your book and gather price quotes from the appropriate sources.

Non-Traditional Methods

Industry pricing standards for e-books are still evolving. Pricing strategies may vary by publisher and many have less than two years' experience publishing e-books. Many experts agree that e-books should be priced significantly less than printed books. Converting a printed book to an electronic file is relatively inexpensive and the middle person (distributor, publisher, printers, bookstore, and wholesaler) can be eliminated, thus reducing production costs and increasing profits.

If you want to sell your books on e-bookstore web sites, the cost for converting your book into an e-book and royalty rates or discounts given to the online e-bookstores will be major costs to consider. Currently, some e-book publishers do not charge a fee for file conversions because they want content to sell to consumers. In the future, we expect e-book publishers will become much more selective on content and will charge more frequently for their conversion services. However, all of them will take a percentage of sales ranging from 30% to 60%. You must carefully consider these costs before committing to the online bookseller.

Some e-publishers will not accept books that have not been professionally edited. Some e-publishers want marketing strategies from the author/publisher before accepting their books. Carefully analyze and shop around for the right e-book publisher for your book.

If you want to test whether your book will sell, then consider print-on-demand (POD) as an alternative printing option. The cost per book will be higher than traditional printing, (e.g. $6 to $12), but the initial printing costs should be lower. This is possible because after PDF or other file formats are set up, you can purchase as little as one book at a time. POD can be an effective marketing strategy for first-time authors who have limited resources. The same advice applies for gathering quotes from various printers, particularly those with digital printing capabilities. Get several quotes and be sure you understand their contract. Another important question to ask when researching printers is what is the process time for completing and delivering your books to your customer. The ideal time should be within one week. However, if they accept the entire book project from editing to cover design, the turnaround can be a few months.

If you are converting your book to a CD-ROM format, contact those publishers with that capability and price it accordingly. Several of the e-book publishers have the ability to convert to CD-ROM. You may also consider adding sound to it. Check our web site www.writershelpdesk.com for a current list of e-book and POD service providers.

Traditional Methods (off-set press printing)

The first step to establishing the cost of your book will require getting quotes from book printers. Notice, we said book printer and not just any printer because there is a big difference between them. Every printer is not qualified to print books. Always ask printers how many books they have printed and ask to see samples of them. Check to see how long they have been printing books and ask references to contact regarding their satisfaction after the books left the printer. If the printer seems apprehensive regarding these questions, be extremely cautious! Recognize printer equipment impacts the quotes they give. Some presses are faster and more efficient than others. Therefore, a printer with the most modern equipment will probably be able to give a lower quote. Ask the printer for a quote sheet to complete. This form is commonly called a RFQ or request for quotation. Most book printers have RFQs prepared with questions that provide them with the necessary information needed for a price estimate. If you have any questions about this form, printers are usually very willing to explain them.

Let's suppose that your book has 100 pages, a full color cover, black text, no photographs and 8 ½ x 11 perfect bound. You plan to sell your book for $9.95. You submit your quote sheet to 20 printers and decide on a printer. You must then add to your printing costs any other expenses directly related to producing your book. Such costs will include editing, book cover design, planned book giveaways, consultant fees, attorney fees, packaging, advertising, etc.

One important factor impacting your costs will be the type of paper stock used in your book. Paper can account up to 50% of your printing costs. The heavier grade of paper will be more expensive than the traditional paper stock. Paper prices will vary drastically because of many factors affecting the forestry industry and tree production. Your price quote can change from one month to another. That's the reason most printers will only guarantee their prices for one month. Paper sells by the pound or weight. Standard paperweight for books range from white or natural offset 50-60# (lb) paper. Paperback novels are usually printed on 33# (lb) novel news paper stock. Hard cover books use heavier paper for quality and longevity. Remember, some small books can be printed on heavier paper and larger font size to appear larger than the actual size.

Another factor that increases your cost of printing will be color printing, inside the book and the cover. Color printing is very expensive, especially with photographs and illustrations. Many colorful books, coffee table books, and illustrated children's books are printed in the Far East due to high cost of color printing in the States. Visit a bookstore and look on the copyright page of the colorfully printed books and notice where it was printed. We list a publishing expert with Asian printer contacts in our Appendix under book packager. Additional Asian printer contacts or brokers may be found in *Literary Market Place.*

If you really feel you have the skills to do most of these tasks yourself, then your profits on your first run should be greater than average. However, do not take these tasks lightly. They are vital to the overall success of your book. Some printers will provide services such as book cover design or minor consulting free or for a small charge. If you feel you need some of these services, then pursue the best source possible. Your budget will influence what you do yourself versus what you pay someone to do.

Many professionals are willing to barter their services. For example, an editor could offer to edit a book if the author could assist with designing their web site in lieu of payment. Ask your accountant about bartering; there may be tax implications.

It's very awkward to edit your own work because you are too close to the subject. Remember the old saying, *'physician heal thyself.'* That's easy to say but difficult to do. However, consider using a professional for some of these services.

Now use the table to determine your cost per book.

Costs	500	1,000	2,000	5,000
Printing	$2,277.00	$2,545.00	$2,931.00	$4,451.00
Cover Design	600.00	600.00	600.00	600.00
Editing	325.00	325.00	325.00	325.00
Layout	500.00	500.00	500.00	500.00
Indexing	250.00	250.00	250.00	250.00
Total Costs	$3,952.00	$4,220.00	$4,606.00	$6,126.00
Cost Per Book*	$7.90	4.22	$2.30	$1.23

See sample form at the end of the chapter.

*Cost per book equals total costs divided by the number of books printed. For example, the cost of $7.90 per book was determined by dividing the total cost figure of $3,952.00 by 500 (books).

In this example, it is unlikely you can charge eight times your cost at the low-end production levels, i.e., 500-1,000. However, you may not need to be concerned with this on your first run since you can test the waters on your first run. At this point, you will be more concerned about the public reaction to your book than your level of profit. Let's face it, even if you could get your cost low enough to price your book at 20 times markup, it means nothing if your book doesn't sell!

Additionally, the way you choose to sell your book will determine the amount of profit. You can compensate for higher production costs by using some of the more profitable ways of selling your book. Again, these methods will be discussed in more detail in Chapter 7. Finally, remember that your second print run should cost significantly less because the printer has already charged you for production layout, filming, plates, etc.

Primary Sales Distribution Channels

Effective distribution of your book is a very critical factor in successfully marketing your book. It can be a nightmare if you try to do it on your own. It's an expensive but very necessary part of doing business. It's easy to think you can fill all the orders yourself from across the country at first thought. However, ask yourself, what if everyone ordered your book on the same day! The post office or express courier service could become your second home.

The book industry has established several primary sales distribution channels for publishers to get their books to the bookstores and libraries. They are called distributors and wholesalers. The term distributor is commonly used but has a distinctive role in getting your book to the public. Since the terms are often misused, we developed a chart to help explain the differences between a distributor and a wholesaler. To add to the confusion, some companies act as both depending on the client or publisher. Remember, books are *not sold* to a distributor or wholesaler, but they are *sold through* them to the consumer. You will need one of them to represent your books with national bookstores.

If you are considering selling your book to libraries, avoid fill in the blank pages. Many libraries will not purchase books that contain them. Library patrons will write in the fill in the blank pages of the book, decreasing the book's shelf life. Baker & Taylor is a national wholesaler that caters to the library market. A few distributors sell exclusively to the library market and you should contact them. We listed them in our reference section. Quality Books is a library distributor and they can provide P-CIP information for your book that is discussed in Chapter 5. They were extremely helpful in preparing our second edition for libraries.

Our chart only covers general policies and pricing. You should contact the firms to gather current policy and pricing information since they are subject to change without notice. You can find more firms in the reference section.

Wholesaler and Distributor Role Distinctions

	Wholesalers	Distributors
Publishers	They represent major, small and independent publishers with warehousing facilities, sales catalogs on a non-exclusive basis	They represent a limited group of publishers with warehousing, sales catalogs and specific sales efforts with an exclusive contract One –two year contract
Sales Team	Limited external sales force selling services and programs to publishers through catalogs They offer customer service support to bookstores and libraries.	Extensive sales team that represent your books nationally and regionally to major bookstore chains & wholesalers. Some may offer sales staff to service territories and key accounts.
Sales Territory	They have centralized buying and regionally selling through their regional warehouses.	They sell nationally usually from one warehouse.
Inventory/Returns	They purchase and stock inventory on as needed basis for order fulfillment. They will return your books after non-activity over a period.	They take your books as inventory on a consignment basis. They will pre-sell new books. They will return your books after non-activity for a period.
Role/Function	They want to fill orders for books quickly to bookstores and libraries.	They want to actively sell your books/titles to bookstores.
Examples	Ingram, Baker & Taylor, Book House	Partners Group, LPC Group, IPG, Bookworld
Discount Rate	55-60%	65-70%

Discounts

Discounts are a necessary part of marketing your book. However, discounts can take away a substantial part of your profits. You should aim for a balance of distribution channels to bring up your profit margins. In other words, diversifying the ways you sell your book will enable you to make more money. Generally, you can count on giving discounts on the various distribution channels as follows:

Sales Channels	Discount	Sales Channels	Discount
Distributors	65%-70%	Wholesalers	55%-60%
Bookstores	40%-50%	Mail Orders	0%
Seminars	0%	Retail Stores	50%
Web site	0%	Online Bookstores	40%-60%
Corporations	0%	Speaking Events	0-50%
Multi-level	0%-70%	Book Clubs/Catalogs	40%-70%

Review our matrix based on assumptions to reach an estimate of sales and profit. You can get an estimate of your book's earnings by using the matrix. We are using a retail price of $9.95 per book.

Sales Channels	Books Sold	Sales	Discount	You Get	Your $$
Wholesaler	400	$3,980.00	55%	45%	$1,791.00
Bookstore	200	$1,990.00	40%	60%	$1,194.00
Mail Order	200	$1,990.00	0%	100%	$1,990.00
Retail Store	200	$1,990.00	50%	50%	$995.00
Totals	1,000	$9,950.00			$5,970.00
Book Production Cost		**Books Produced**		**Cost Per Book**	
$4,220		1,000		$4.22	
Dollars Received (Sales)		**Minus Production Costs**		**Equals Gross Profit**	
$5,970.00		$4,220.00		$1,750.00	

Sample form at the end of the chapter.

In this example, you sold 1,000 books for a total of $9,950 in gross sales (before giving discounts). After giving discounts to the various wholesalers, bookstores and retail stores, you received $5,970.00 or 67% of total sales dollars. From this amount you must deduct any of your expenses related to promoting or selling your book, such as travel, minor advertising, postage, marketing materials, etc. However, if you manage your expenses right, you should be able to earn more than the 5%-15% royalties from a publisher.

In the above example, profit margins are lower because only 1,000 books are used in the example. Production costs per book are much higher for short runs or small quantity productions. Also, the example includes costs that only occur on the first production run, such as editing, layout, indexing, and cover design. As production numbers increase, costs per book decrease and profit margins increase significantly.

This example does not take into account *when* you receive your money. Do not expect to receive all your money right away. For example, wholesalers can take up to 120 days to pay you! Worst of all, you may not get paid at all, depending upon the character or financial strength of the company to which you extend credit. When you don't get paid right away, you must decide whether you want to trust the party to pay you later. This is called making a credit decision or extending credit. Don't make this decision lightly when you are dealing with small or unknown companies. You have risks with well-known companies as well, but not as much as dealing with small, unscrupulous, or financially unstable companies. So, check out the wholesalers, distributors, and stores *before* you trust them with your books. Remember, we mentioned ways to check out companies in Chapter 2.

Publishing Cost and Profits

Costs	500	1,000	2,500	5,000	10,000
Printing					
Cover Design					
Editing					
Layout					
Indexing					
Total Costs					
Cost Per Book					

Total Book Production Costs

Sales Channels	Books Sold	Sales	Discount	You Get	Your $$
Wholesaler					
Bookstore					
Mail Order					
Retail Store					
Totals					
Book Production Cost		Books Produced		Cost Per Book	
Dollars Received (Sales)		Minus Production Costs		Equals Gross Profit	

Gross Dollar Profit

Chapter 4

Setting Up Your Publishing Company

"Everything big starts with something little!"

By now you have priced your book, determined the cost of producing your book, given some thought to how you will sell your book and decided to move forward with your book project. It's now a good time to discuss establishing your self-publishing business.

Naming Your New Company

Give some thought to naming your company. Even if you only plan to publish one book, spend some time with this task. A sure sign of an amateur is to use the word "enterprises" in your company name. You might want to use publishing or publishers in your company name, but it is not necessary. We do not generally recommend using your personal name as part of your business name. Many book reviewers still do not believe most self-publishers are credible. If you name your company like an amateur, they probably won't take you seriously. Make your name simple, easy to remember but keep it professional.

You should consider creating a company logo especially when you have your cover designed. The logo simply lends more credibility to your company. Over time, it could add value to your company as a recognizable trademark. A logo can simply be a unique font (type) for naming your company or it can contain graphics. Graphic designers for your book cover can assist you with creating a logo or you can use computer software to create your own. An art school, institute, or colleges are other sources for help with logos at a reasonable price.

Sales Tax License

If you plan to sell your books yourself, you should get a sales tax license. Contact local branches or state offices for information on laws for where you plan to conduct business. In Texas, contact the State of Texas -The Comptroller of Public Accounts at (800) 252-5555 for more information. You can also search the Internet and your state's web site for sales tax information.

Choosing a Business Form

Sole Proprietorship

A sole proprietorship is exactly what the name implies, one owner. It is very simple to form a sole proprietorship. In Texas, all you have to do is confirm at the county clerk's office that no other company has filed the same name. You then can apply for an Assumed Name Certificate or D.B.A. (Doing Business As). You may contact your local county clerk's office for more information.

This form of business does not protect you from litigation as a corporation would. If your business is sued, you are sued personally. However, business liability insurance is an alternative to consider.

Liability insurance may be available through some professional associations, such as the *Publishers Marketing Association* (see the Resource Guide at the end of book*)*.

General Partnership

A general partnership can be an answer to a prayer or your worst nightmare. Many individuals form partnerships to pool their resources for a common cause. Each partner is legally responsible for what the other does. Each partner is jointly and severally responsible for the liabilities of the partnership. In other words, creditors or other entities can sue each partner personally. In addition, one partner can create problems for *all* the partners. Trust and harmony is vital in a general partnership. Before you get involved with this form of business, you should be sure you know all the risks involved. A general partnership is often termed a professional marriage. As with any marriage, you can expect a few disagreements or conflicts.

If your partnership runs into credit problems, creditors will often go after the strongest partner. This partner may end up suing you to recover personal losses, even though the creditor has already filed suit against you. Again, seek professional advice before you enter into any agreement, *written* or *oral*.

Limited Partnership

A limited partnership is also another way to pool resources for a business venture. The investors are the limited partners and their personal liability is limited to their financial investment. A general partner is the party that puts the deal together and usually operates the business venture. Limited partnerships are common investment vehicles for real estate and oil and gas deals.

This form of business can be complicated and it is wise to consult a CPA, tax attorney or other qualified source *before* signing any agreement. It is *not* a common way to start a publishing business.

Corporation

A major advantage of a corporation is the protection it affords you from personal litigation or liability. When you form a corporation, the corporation is treated as a separate entity. The owner or owners of the corporation have limited liability.

Shares of stock are issued to the owner or owners of the corporation. If one of the shareholders dies, the corporation continues to operate. One disadvantage of a corporation is the potential of double taxation. The corporation is taxed on its profits and the shareholders are taxed on any dividends.

Subchapter S Corporation

Subchapter S Corporations or S Corps make it possible for small businesses to avoid double taxation. Once a corporation is formed, the shareholders file a Subchapter S election with the IRS. When this is approved, profits or losses can flow directly through the corporation to the shareholders. In other words, the shareholders are taxed instead of the corporation. The shareholders simply list their share of the profits or losses on their personal tax returns.

There are several restrictions to S Corps. Check with an attorney or CPA to assist you with this type of corporation. Some government agencies, such as the Small Business Administration, may have free brochures or booklets that cover this form of business.

Limited Liability Company

The limited liability company (LLC) is a relatively new business form. It has several advantages over other business forms. For example, although they may operate like a traditional partnership, the owners have certain privileges similar to corporations. An LLC is taxed as a partnership, allowing losses or profits to pass on or flow through to the individual owners. Additionally, liabilities are limited, giving owners some protection from being sued individually for liabilities of the business. Setting up this form of business generally requires an attorney to draft the necessary legal documents for you. Many professionals and companies that are concerned about business liabilities find an LLC appealing.

Laws change periodically and controls on this form of business may tighten or loosen in the future. Consequently, as in all forms of businesses, you should seek the advice of a professional on whether this form of business is right for you.

Chapter 5

Before You Publish Your Book...

"Begin with the end in mind." ... Stephen Covey

Before you send your manuscript to be published, there are several things you must do or obtain to protect your work and position your book professionally. These important details are: copyright, ISBN, bar code, Library of Congress Catalog Card Number, and Cataloging in Publication.

Copyright

A copyright serves to protect your work from being reproduced or copied by others without your permission. Today, your writings are automatically covered under current copyright law. However, you are encouraged to register your work with The Copyright Office of the Library of Congress. Copyrights afford you certain rights in the event you have to sue to protect your work. Seek an attorney on this subject and be sure to select one that specializes in copyright law. Attorney referral web sites and links are listed in the Resource Guide. Also, the address and phone number of the Copyright Office is provided. The Copyright Office can provide you with *free* material that explains your rights and the necessary application forms. A sample of the form used to register your book is listed in the Appendix. You should print the copyright information on the back of the title page of your book and file Form TX or Short Form TX *shortly after* the book is published. An example of the copyright information is ©2001 Your Company Name or Your Name. The general information web site address for the Library of Congress: http://lcweb.loc.gov/ then click copyright or other areas of interest.

ISBN

You must also obtain an International Standard Book Number (ISBN). This number is an identification number for your book that is ultimately published in *Books in Print,* an important source book stores and others use to order books. The ISBN should appear on the copyright page of your book and on the bottom of the back cover or dust jacket, usually above the bar code. Bookstores, wholesalers, and distributors require this number for inventory and pricing data. Be sure to get an ISBN *before* you print your book.

The U.S. agency licensed to sell the ISBN is R.R. Bowker. A set of 10 numbers currently costs $225.00 for normal delivery service (about three weeks) with an additional charge for rush 72-hour service. A sample of the ISBN application is listed in the Appendix.

Some vendors may offer to sell a single ISBN that was issued to them for a fraction of the cost of buying 10 numbers. We recommend you buy your own full set of numbers. If you are using another company's number, a book wholesaler or distributor will probably not stock your book. This presents a major problem if you want to sell your books in chain bookstores. Wholesalers and distributors are discussed in detail in Chapter 7.

Standard Address Number (SAN)

A SAN is a unique seven-digit identifying number used to indicate a specific address of a company directly or indirectly related to the publishing industry. R.R. Bowker, the same agency that sells the ISBN, assigns it. Many wholesalers and distributors recommend that you get this number, although it is currently optional. A SAN serves to sort billing and shipping addresses and help organize order processing.

Advance Book Information (ABI)

This form provides all the details about your book such as book size, number of pages, type of binding, number of editions, pricing, genres, etc. The information on the Advance Book Information (ABI) form is then listed in *Books in Print*. It is completed *after* you receive the ISBN numbers. You will assign an ISBN number. We suggest you select one in the middle of the ten numbers. Oftentimes, novices pick the first number on the list, ending with an *x'*. Seasoned publishing experts can tell that's the first book by looking at the number that ends in *'x.'* Please remember the *publication date* requested on this form is the date you plan to initiate major marketing and promotion of your published book. The date your book is published does not have to coincide with the publication date (publicity campaign launch date).

How to File

Write or call the ISBN Agency and request an application for an *ISBN Publisher Prefix,* an instruction manual, and an Advance Book Information *(ABI)* Form. Examples of these forms are located in the Resource Guide at the end of this book. The address is as follows:

ISBN U.S. Agency
R.R. Bowker
121 Chanlon Road
New Providence, NJ 07974
Ph: 908-665-6770
Fax: 908-665-2895
www.bowker.com

You may also apply online as follows:
ISBN: www.bowker.com/standards/home/isbn/us/application.html
ABI: www.bowkerlink.com/corrections/bip/itemsearch.asp

Bookland EAN Bar Code

The Bookland EAN bar code is the standard bar code for books. Bar codes are a requirement for your book and appear on the back cover. Bar codes contain numbers that identify the publisher, author, book price, edition, etc. Today most bookstores have scanners and will want a bar code on your book for convenience and inventory control. Some larger bookstores will also add their own bar code label to your book. Sources for bar codes are listed in the Resource Guide. You should request the Bookland EAN bar code with price code. You must also include the ISBN, author, publisher, price, etc.

Scanners work best when bar codes are printed on white backgrounds with black ink. Other dark color ink on light color backgrounds will work, but be sure to check them out with your bar code vendor first. Fotel, a bar code firm, provides a detailed explanation of bar codes on its web site at www.fotel.com. Another source of information is *Machine Readable Coding Guidelines for the U.S. Book Industry.* Published by the Book Industry Study Group, this publication explains Bar Code printing rules in detail. You may contact them at (212) 929-1393 to purchase the pamphlet for $7.50 or order it online at www.bisg.org/pub.html

UPC Bar Code

If you plan to publish a mass-market book, you may also need to have a Universal Product Code (UPC). Grocery, drug, and discount stores may require you to add their industry code or a UPC bar code. Some of these retailers may want you to also add the Bookland EAN Bar Code on the inside front cover of your book. It's a good idea to check with them on their requirements *before* you print your book. A list of bar code companies is included in the Appendix.

Library of Congress Catalog Card Number (LCCN)

If you plan to market your book to libraries, your book must be assigned a Library of Congress Card Number or LCCN You only have to request one number for each book title, regardless of how many times you revise your book. However, you must also request this number *before* your book goes to print. This number must appear on the copyright page of your book. There are certain restrictions to assignment of numbers. For example, if your book is less than 50 pages and not a children's book or genealogy, it is not eligible for a number.

Cataloging In Publication (CIP) And Publishers-Cataloging In Progress (P-CIP)

This program makes it easier for librarians to purchase, process, and place new titles on the shelf location for books based on their subject matter. CIP contains technical data, including the ISBN, Dewey and Library of Congress classification numbers, and Library of Congress subject classifications. This information is listed on the copyright page on your book.

In order to be accepted in this program, you should have at least three books already published. You may contact the CIP directly for more information at (202) 707-6372 or write to CIP Office, Library of Congress, Washington, DC 20540. They have a publication, "Cataloging in Publication—Information", you may find useful. You may also visit their web site at http://lcweb.loc.gov/loc/infopub.

If all your books are self-published, you will not qualify unless you publish other author's books. However, you have another option. Quality Books, Inc., a major library book distributor, can provide a Publisher's Cataloging in Publication (P-CIP).

Quality Books will catalog your new title for as little as $40.00 and mail you a camera-ready copy. If you want to receive this information within 10 business days, you can pay an express service fee of $75.00. Fees may change contact them for a price. Quality

Books is located at 1003 W. Pines Road, Oregon, IL 61061-9680. You may contact Jane Griswold at (815) 732-4450 or (800) 323-4241. If you prefer you may e-mail her at Jane.Griswold@dawson.com or fax her at (815) 732-4499. Their web site address is www.quality-books.com. An application is required and you must already have the ISBN and LCCN information before they can catalog your title.

Applying

To apply for a *free* preassigned LCCN, call the Library of Congress at (202) 707-6372, and ask for the *Request for Preassignment of Library of Congress Catalog Card Number* (Form 607-7). You can also apply online. *A*lso, ask for any instruction material that can help you complete the form. Online application is available at their web site at:

http://pcn.loc.gov/pcn

Alternatively, if you prefer, you can write to request the form and other information at:

Library of Congress
Cataloging in Publication Division
101 Independence Ave., S.E.
Washington, DC 20540-4320

The completed application should be typed. A copy of the book's title page should be sent with the application and a copy of the published book should be sent to the Library of Congress.

It is important to apply in this order:

1. Apply for the ISBN
2. Apply for LCCN or P-CIP (if you want libraries to buy your book)
3. Send ABI Form
4. Copyright (after the books are printed-send 2 copies)

Common Mistakes

We offer a warning of advice regarding the common mistakes made by new authors. If you are reading our book before you publish your book, or you have already published book, please pay close attention to our list.

Common mistakes to avoid as a new author:

• Trying to do everything yourself or not listening to someone in a position to know more than you.

• Failure to join or participate in writers' organizations.

• Failure to attend publishing and writing events/conferences.

• Editing the book yourself.

•Failing to attend training seminars given by experts in your industry.

• Paying far too much for a service because you did not get enough quotes.

• Thinking a vanity publisher is the same as a traditional publisher or book printer.

• Failure to identify your target audience.

• Failing to check out a printer before you spend your money.

• Pricing your book insufficiently to cover your expenses and ensure profitability.

• Setting a price for your book that is unrealistic or far higher, or even lower, than similar books.

• Failing to research your competition before you spend all your money.

• Failing to develop a marketing plan before you spend your money.

• Dropping the ball on promoting your book once it is in bookstores. Overcoming the fear of public speaking through practice and training.

• Not knowing bookstores will return your books if they don't sell fast enough.

• Spending all your profits on personal needs.

• Assigning a copyright year that is much older than the print date. (e.g. book printed in 2001, but copyright date 2000)

Don't be overwhelmed with the prospect of making a mistake on your first book. Because you are reading this book, you are obviously a person committed to making your book project a success. Go to the resource section and read as much material as possible on publishing and marketing your book. Check out www.writershelpdesk.com. It is complete with information you will need during your journey to successfully completing your book project. Our book can prevent you from making some of those common mistakes by new authors.

Chapter 6

Designing Your Book To Sell

"Do not let what you cannot do interfere with what you can do."

John Wooden

Make no mistake about this fact - you *can* tell a book by its cover! Your book *will* be judged by its cover! If someone notices your book on a shelf, you have less than 30 seconds to sell it. Studies reveal that the average person will spend 10 seconds on the front and 15 seconds reading the back cover. Your book cover is a significant sales tool. You can write the greatest book but if it's packaged with an ugly book cover, it will not sell! The cover is a vital part of your advertising efforts. Often, it is your most important sales aid in a bookstore. Since you only have a few seconds to impress the customer, you must invest time, energy, and/or money on this selling tool. If you can afford it, using a graphic artist experienced in designing book covers is highly recommended.

Book Basics

The Library of Congress qualifies a book as 49 pages or greater, regardless of page size, and that includes blank pages! Therefore, your book can be any size you want. Stop thinking you need 700 pages for a book.

Every book should have a category or genre. Genre is a marketing term that categorizes books for store placement. A book can be categorized as mainstream fiction, romance, sci-fi, mystery, thrillers, Western, horror, historical, literary novels, and children's books. There are two types of books, fiction, and non-fiction. Fiction is a made up story, invented, even if it's based on actual events. Non-fiction is based on truth, expert opinion, or research. Non-fiction books are biographies, how-to books, true crime, reference, cookbooks, travel, pop culture, humor, health, inspirational, religious, new age, children's books, business, and memoirs. Poetry is one of the most difficult to sell because it's hard to define. A poet's best investment is the *Poet's Market* by *Writer's Digest*, it's filled with a wealth of resources. Your book must fulfill one of these three fundamental needs from the reader's perspective; *inspire them, inform them, or entertain them.* It is possible to meet all three but at least one must be fulfilled.

Fiction books can have three formats, short story, novella, and novel. A short story is less than 30 manuscript pages, novellas can be 30-150 manuscript pages, and a novel can be 250 manuscript pages or greater.

All odd numbered pages are on the right and even numbered pages are on the left. Chapters should begin on the right hand side or odd numbered pages. Blank pages are counted in the total number of pages. Page numbers do not have to appear on all pages. One of your best investments as a writer and publisher should be *The Chicago Manual of Style - The Essential Guide for Writers, Editors & Publishers.* This book will address every formatting concern or question.

Front Cover Tips (AKA Book Jacket)

The front cover title of your book should stand out from the rest of the print. A subtitle should be used to further describe the subject matter of the book, if needed. For example, our book *Turning Stones Into Gems* could be confused with a book on jewelry or magic. However, the subtitle clarifies the purpose of the book by describing the subject matter of the book. The front cover should also include the name of the author and may have a strong endorsement or book review or mention the name of a prestigious award. According to studies, women buy more books than men (more than 80% of book buyers). Your book cover should appeal to women, even if your target audience is men. Women will buy the book to give to men.

Use Contrast

Contrast helps to get your book noticed. Examples of suggestions for contrast are:

> Use lighter background with darker color type or darker background with lighter color type.

> Use different type (font) and styles for the title and subtitle.

> Use upper and lowercase letter combinations.

> Use regular type, italics and bold typeface combinations.

Back Cover Tips

The back cover should contain the benefits of the book, endorsements and testimonials, the book subject category, bar code, ISBN, name, publisher information, book price, and web site address (if available). The bar code includes the suggested retail price of the book and ISBN. We recommend printing the Canadian price on the back along with the US price. The Canadian price is approximately 40% more. A photograph of the author is optional. Most readers want to know something about the author; a photo allows the reader to relate to the author. We put our picture on our cover so our readers will know we are ordinary people trying to help others achieve their dreams.

Spine

For many books, the spine is the first part of the book the reader will see on the shelf. Display the author's name and the title prominently so they're easy to read. Use a simple and easy to read font. No need to get too fancy here because the human eye may not focus on it well. Don't risk losing a potential buyer because they can't read the fancy script. Use your publisher logo if it's eye-catching. Printing the full company name here is not necessary, depending on the thickness of the spine. Consider stacking the title name to make it more noticeable.

Book Binding

Binding your book is a critical part of packaging your book. Various types of binding are available depending on your budget. Perfect binding is the common and popular form of book binding that is glued on soft cover books. Your book spine must be legible when stacked on the bookshelves. Your book should be a minimum 50 pages to meet this requirement.

Perfect binding is the most economical and practical for many books. Case binding, hardcover, or cloth binding is usually sewn, or side stitched and then glued between hard cardboards. Hardcover books are expensive to manufacture and are priced accordingly. Hardcover books are reviewed more than others, garner a lot of press, and carry prestige for the author. Most bestsellers and academic books are hardbacks. Hardcover books usually sell less than any other books unless it makes a bestseller list. The average hardcover novel will sell from 3,000 – 10,000 copies versus mass market novels sell from 25,000- 100,000 copies. We discuss book lengths and sizes further in this chapter. Book pricing is a major factor for those sales. Paperback novels (mass market) usually sell for $6.00 or less and hardcover novels sell for $20.00 or more.

Mechanical binding is the type of binding used with digital printing such as Docu-Tech® on print-on-demand books. Plastic comb and spiral wire binding is used for workbooks, manuals, and cookbooks that can lay flat. Otabind® is another form of comb binding that is better because printing can be placed on the spine. Books with Otabind® lay flat. Our successful first edition of *How to Self-Publish & Market Your Own Book* was plastic comb binding. You can bind a book using an inexpensive comb-binding machine especially if you use the books in workshops. Wire stitching and saddle stitching are used for booklets and pamphlets less than 80 pages. They are stapled on the inside or outside of the booklet.

Bookstores highly prefer perfect bound and hardback books because they are stacked spine out on the bookshelves. Libraries prefer hardcover books because of durability. If your book sells, the bookstore and library will carry them regardless of your binding.

Other Tips

Research other books in your category or genre

Visit bookstores and browse for book cover ideas. Pay attention to why you select certain books based on their covers. Your cover should match the energy your book evokes from the reader. For example, if you are writing something positive and uplifting, don't have your cover dark and dreary looking because black or gray is your favorite color. Some printers have generic design templates or samples that you can review and select for your book A few large printers may have custom cover design services for a fee. The extra time and effort you spend on your book cover can make the difference between success and failure for your book if you sell it primarily in bookstores.

Design your book to be noticed

Research other books in your book's genre for design ideas. Try to make your book stand out from the crowd. Try different sizes, graphics, font, colors, etc. If you have a great endorsement, award, or review, consider putting it on the front cover. Your book usually should be compatible with other books in the same genre. For example, a paperback romance novel has a standard format, size,

(4.25" x 7") front cover, etc. You would not expect to see a paperback romance novel without a picture on the front and in the 8.5" x 11" format. However, sometimes an odd size will get your book noticed and enhance sales. Our point is that you have to use good judgment, however don't be afraid to test the waters. If you are trying something totally radical, you might start with a short run of books first. If you are satisfied with the sales results, then print a larger amount of books the next time. You will spend a little more money this way, but you could save a lot too if the response to your book idea was unfavorable.

Book Sizes and Length

Your book size will impact your printing costs. Book formats usually fall into several categories. Remember, the more paper needed for your book, the more costly to print it. The formats of book sizes usually fall into categories according to the market.

📖	4.25" x 7"	Mass markets (novels)
📖	5.50" x 8.50"	Tradebook, fiction, non-fiction
📖	6" x 9"	Tradebook, fiction, non-fiction
📖	7" x 9	Textbook, manual
📖	9" x 12"	Coffee table book
📖	7.50" x 9	Gift book, art book
📖	8.50" x 11	Manual, workbook, textbook

The length of your book can be difficult to determine until you have finished your manuscript. Do not try to guess total page count because the number of pages will determine most of your costs. The number of pages in your double spaced manuscript does not equal your book page total. Your book will usually be one third less the size of your manuscript. The standard ratio of manuscript pages to book pages is 1.5 double-spaced 8.5 " x 11" manuscript pages to one 5.50" x 8.50" book page. For example, your manuscript is 338 pages is divided by 1.5 equals 225 book pages sized at 5.50" x 8.50".

You can also format your book page format on your word processor and copy and paste ten pages of your manuscript on the formatted page. You can use that multiple to determine your page count. Most word processors allow you to customize any book dimension to a page acceptable for your printer.

Remember, most books are single-spaced or a space and one half. Your manuscript is double-spaced. The final formatting and layout of your book could increase your pages slightly after you add footers, headers, and pagination. A proper formatted manuscript is double-spaced and 12 point size preferably Times New Roman font on 8.5 " x 11"page.

Use of Colors

Learn which colors invoke particular emotions from people. Colors can convey deeper meaning that can go beyond pleasing the eye. For example, blue means cool and conveys calmness and tranquility. Blue can be appealing to busy, hurried readers. Purple conveys royalty, elegance, spirituality, and creativity. Red is a hot color that expresses passion, action, and a high level of seriousness. Yellow is a warm color that means happiness, inquisitive, and optimistic. Pink conveys romantic, sensitive, beauty, and feminism. Green implies prosperity, healing, intelligence, and luck. The composition of your target audience will determine the colors you select for your cover such as young single women, baby boomers, adolescents, children, etc. A helpful web site on colors and book cover designs is bookcovers.com listed under our resources

Use full or four-color process covers

Color attracts attention and that's what you want. Although color is more expensive, this can be money well spent. Greater attention and increased sales will justify the additional expense of a full-color book cover. Sometimes a black and white or two-color cover can work just as well as a full-color cover. For example, if you are selling your book in seminars, people are more interested in the information than the packaging.

Keep it simple and avoid clutter

If your book is on a shelf, the title should be easy to read from a distance. The theme of the cover should be easy to understand. Too many graphics and words on the cover will probably prompt a reader to move to another book. So keep it simple, but make it grab their attention. Remember, great artwork on a wall may not translate well on a 6 x 9 book cover!

Design a cover that fits your audience

If you are producing a cookbook, your cover should have a food item. If your book is on fishing, it might help to have a picture of a fish on the cover. If you are writing a romance novel, a sensuous picture of a man and woman on the cover would not hurt. Our point is you should use common sense. You have already done your research with other book covers in your book's genre. Gather ideas from the bestsellers in your category. Also, remember women buy the majority of books, whether for themselves or for a man. Make sure your cover grabs women's attention if you want them to buy it.

A good book cover designer is worth the expense

Don't take lightly the value of a book cover. Expect to pay from $600 to $3,000. Some publishers have oil paintings done from which they run prints for the cover. Expect to spend at least five figures if you get this elaborate. Self-publishers don't need to spend this kind of money to be successful. However, using a relative or a best friend to design your cover may not get you the results you need.

Our graphic designer listened to our ideas on a cover concept. She also read our galley before she designed drafts of the cover. She knew what size font to use on the spine based on the number of pages in our book. She knew which printers were good with color separation. She had the latest software and an arsenal of graphic tools. She saved us a lot of time and trouble because she specialized in book covers. She was well worth the investment we made in our book cover.

When you are proud of the appearance of your book, it shows when you talk about it. People can see and hear your enthusiasm. You may have a great book, but if you hate the cover you may reflect your dissatisfaction or frustration when you are promoting your book. This is not to say you are guaranteed success because you have a great cover. However, great covers sell books. What's inside the book counts more, but a well-designed cover will get the reader to pick up your book from the shelf. If you sell your book in bookstores, you need to take the book cover seriously. Book cover designers are listed in our Appendix.

Chapter 7

Promoting And Marketing Your Book

Friends may ask, "What if it doesn't work?" But you ask, "What if it does?"

In this chapter, you become acquainted with some of the ways to promote and market your book. Since this will be a major factor in the success of your book, pay close attention to these suggestions. How you use this publicity information will determine whether your book becomes a success or failure.

There are many ways to promote your book that will not require a major expense, so you don't have to focus on traditional advertising. Why is this important? Advertising is paid for and publicity is free! The budget of a self-publisher is generally too small to justify spending much money on popular advertising media, such as radio, television, and national magazine display ads. You should learn as much as you can about marketing. Go to the library and find the books recommended in this book. Research and read all you can about the publishing industry.

First, join a trade organization/association in your area. Most cities have at least one writer's group that meets monthly. They usually sponsor a conference or seminar annually that covers publicity and marketing. You should make plans to attend seminars and workshops offered in your city. You can find more writing events on our web site - www.writershelpdesk.com.. Ask your friends, co-workers, and relatives about book club meetings and offer your book as a selection to read and discuss. Find a mentor who can answer your questions and encourage you. Remember, no one will know your book is a bestseller until you learn how to sell it to your target audience.

Learning about free and inexpensive ways to promote your book through publicity will help successfully increase your book sales. Ask your printer for an extra 100 copies of your book cover to use with your promotional campaign. You will also explore the various distribution channels or ways you can market your book.

Publicity

Janice Gibson, President of Three G Communications located in Houston, Texas, defines publicity as "the use of non-paid time and space in media outlets to garner interest and create awareness". Publicity for your book is achieved through tools such as news releases, book reviews, radio interviews, television interviews seminars, speaking engagements and book signings.

News Releases

One of the most inexpensive ways to generate publicity is through a news release. The broader term news release is preferred to press release because certain media cannot be limited to the term "press". Common targets for new releases are newspapers, radio, television, and magazines. Use news releases to promote your book signing, seminar, speaking engagements and any other events where you can plug or use excerpts from your book.

Many cities compile media guides or directories listing the names, addresses, phone and fax numbers and contact persons of all the newspapers, radio and television stations. Contact a member of the Society of Professional Journalists for their complete listing. For smaller cities, you can simply contact the local newspapers and stations for the same information. Other sources such as Standard Rate and Data Services (SRDS), *Bacon's Newspaper/Magazine Directory*, *Bacon's Publicity Checker*, *Gale Directory of Publications and Broadcast Media* can be found in your local library. These reference books cover every major city and will provide useful demographic information such as the audience, format, reach, frequency, etc.

What to Write in the News Release

If you are having an event, simply describe it. Be sure to state *who, what, when, where,* and *why* information. If you are announcing your new book, give the features and benefits of your book. Try to tie in a local angle, current event, trend, or situation to your book. For example, U R Gems Group wrote a news release that featured the low unemployment rate to announce a career development seminar. The news release focused on the benefits of attending the seminar. The news release became very effective and successful in our city and other cities because we didn't feature our book, *Turning Stones Into Gems*. The largest paper ran the release in several different sections. Incidentally, smaller cities will be more likely to run your entire release since they are always looking for fillers. Larger cities tend to edit your release for basic information due to limited space.

We recommend you read books on publicity, attend classes, checkout the web sites in our reference section. Many community colleges and adult learning centers (i.e. Leisure Learning-Houston, Learning Annex-Los Angeles) offer inexpensive classes on getting publicity and writing news releases taught by professionals. There are web sites that have creative and exciting tips for book promotions and writing effective news releases. A great book on publicity and excellent ideas for news releases is Raleigh Pinskey's, *101 Ways To Promote Yourself & Tricks of the Trade for Taking Charge of Your Own Success.* Her web site is www.promoteyourself.com.

Writing Your News Release

Type "FOR IMMEDIATE RELEASE" at the top left of the page or "FOR RELEASE ON (DATE)" if you want it released during a certain week. Type a date under IMMEDIATE RELEASE. Place at the top right of the page, the name, and number of the person to contact. Use 12-point or larger font size.

Begin with an attention-getting, newsworthy headline. If you don't get the reader's attention in the headline, chances are your news release will get tossed. You need to get a hook! Spend time with writing the headline or the rest of your efforts may be futile. Refer to the discussion on headlines in this chapter.

You should make your release easy to read and edit by using double space or no less than 1.5 spaces between the lines. Use 12-point font in the body of the release and a larger size font (type) in the headline.

Try to limit your release to one or two pages.

The first paragraph should contain the meat and potatoes of your release. Make sure it does not sound like an advertisement. Instead, stress the benefits to the readers and tie it into the headline.

The rest of the news release may provide brief information about the background of the author, your company, etc.

If you have more that one page type *-more-* at the bottom center of each page. End the news release with ### in the center of the bottom of the last page.

Print your media release on the back of your extra book covers if your book size permits. Mail out the releases.

An example of our actual company news release created for our first seminar and book signing follows on the next page. The release ran in our major newspaper, several weekly papers, a popular radio program interview, and several television interviews.

Don't overlook the power of a news release. Often they are more effective than advertising and are inexpensive to produce. Your news release could include tips or a list from your book with brief subject matter covering the topics. Papers looking for filler have printed some writers' news releases. For example, during the month of February, books on relationships, romance, marriage, jewelry, and love can have a hook for Valentine's Day. Learn what days and weeks are recognized as national events by reading *Celebrate Today* by John Kremer (www.bookmarket.com) or contacting your local library.

If you are not getting results from your news releases, you may want to consider consulting a public relations firm. Some firms will work with you on an hourly consulting basis to offer suggestions on how to improve your news releases. Seek out publicists that have authors as clients, so ask other authors for referrals.

FOR IMMEDIATE RELEASE   **Contact:** Sara Freeman Smith
April 2, 1998   281-596-8330

IMAGINE HAVING A VALUABLE GOD GIVEN TALENT . . .
AND NOT KNOWING IT OR USING IT!

Have your parents ever told you to stop wasting your time doing something, because you can't earn a living doing it?

Have you ever felt you were meant to do something better, but didn't know what or how?

Have you ever trained someone who later became your boss?

Well, you are not alone. With unemployment at its lowest level in 25 years, now is an excellent time to begin a new job or career or change jobs and careers. Recognizing that young people and adults need to be encouraged and challenged to think and choose careers for which they have a passion. Motivational trainer and author, Sara Freeman Smith, is giving a free workshop to help you discover your hidden talents, learn how to land a better job or change to a more rewarding career.

Title: **Turning Stones Into Gems™**
When: Saturday, May 2, 1998, 1:00 p.m. - 3:00 p.m.
Where: Main Street Books, 4201 Main Street, Houston, TX
Fee: **Free**

For information call - U R Gems Group - 281- 596-8330

Sara Freeman Smith has inspired and helped hundreds of Houstonians discover how to release their God given talents into productive careers and small businesses. We invite students, parents, adults, unemployed and underemployed to attend. The workshop will inspire you to think out the box and not limit your ability based on your circumstances or other people's opinions. Sara takes this workshop directly from her personal testimony and will cover vital tips outlined in her book, ***Turning Stones Into Gems®.***

#

Announcements

Now that you have your news release, begin to think of individuals you want to tell and invite to your upcoming event. Sending out e-mail announcements can be very quick, efficient, professional, and even personal. You can simply format your announcement nicely in an e-mail and send it to people that you know personally. Use every opportunity to ask for e-mail addresses to alert them of your upcoming events. We don't recommend sending e-mail news releases to the media unless they ask you to do so. Media professionals are bombarded with spam or unsolicited e-mails and they may never see it. We recommend faxing and/or mailing it to the media.

Design your own personal postcard with an invitation to your event, apply a postcard stamp, and mail it. You can purchase custom greeting card software package or use custom formats on your personal software to design your postcard. Some authors design flyers to distribute on car windshields or personally at shopping malls, churches, conventions, and special events. You can hire students or special events teams to distribute them. Always target your event with your audience you want to reach.

We use list servers to send out announcements and they are well received by the members. A list server is group listing of members with a common purpose such as writers groups, books clubs, etc. We use e-Groups.com. You can join certain web sites and they allow you to post upcoming events to the web site. The Internet has several invitation sites that can be used to e-mail announcements such as E-vite.com. Your E-vite invitation will alert you when someone responds to your invitation and save all your e-mail addresses for future use.

Pat G'Orge-Walker, author of *"Ain't Nobody Else Right But Us – All Others Goin' to Hell" Church* (www.sisterbetty.com), a series of gospel comedy short stories, suggests some of her *shameless promotion tactics* she used to promote her books. She recommends you get an Internet provider that offers multiple screen names.

Create several different screen names as individual reviewers for your book or just to announce your new book. Only use these screen names selectively, in discussion groups, chat rooms, etc. when discussing your books. Pat states, "Each one delivers an endorsement worthy of being placed right up there with the creation of air, water, fire and rain!" Track your results by asking how they heard about your book. Remember; always document where you discussed the book and which screen name you used. Pat got an overwhelming response and sales from her *shameless promotion.*

Book Reviews

Book reviews are another inexpensive way to promote your book to potential buyers. Many publications have designated staff that reviews books to mention in future articles. Certain trade magazines review books prior to their publication in order to give bookstores enough time to order the books before they are advertised to consumers. Many online bookstores and writing groups will review your book if it fits their audience. A good review will usually generate sales for your book. Two good sources of book reviews are *Publishers Weekly* and *Library Journal*. The *Writer's Digest Writer's Market* provides detail about book reviewers. Book reviewers are listed in the Resource Guides. Query your favorite web sites where book reviews appear and find out the criteria for reviews.

If you are trying to arouse interest in your book among wholesalers, libraries, distributors and bookstores, you should consider sending galleys to book reviewers. A galley is a pre-publication unedited copy of a book bound for reviewers. A galley is normally sent at least four months *before* the publication date of your book. The publication date is the date you list on the ABI form mentioned in Chapter 5. It is *not* the date your book is printed, but rather the date you plan to launch the major part of your book promotion.

Many reviewers prefer perfect bound galleys. Perfect binding is the glued on type binding used on paperbacks or soft cover books. However, other forms may be acceptable such as plastic comb binding. It's probably best to check with the reviewer for guidelines. Book reviewers want to know why a reader will buy the book. Always focus on the benefits of your book to hook a reviewer or editor. Unfortunately, poor quality books often come from vanity and self-publishers who did not put a lot of thought and effort into their work.

Remember, you are not guaranteed that your book will be reviewed because reviewers receive hundreds of book submissions daily! Your submission letter should be an attention grabber. The two books listed in the Resource Guides that discuss galleys in more detail are *The Self-Publishing Manual* and *The Successful Self-Publisher.*

Radio Talk Shows

Radio interviews are another excellent way to gain exposure. Many stations are constantly looking for interesting people to appear on their talk shows. However, as you begin to expand from local to regional and national promotions, radio interviews can be conducted over the phone. Our preference is for live shows, but they are not always necessary. Prior to visiting a city for your interviews, arrange book signings or seminars to sell your books. You will be able to announce the location and time of your event during the broadcast or print interview and gain further *free* publicity

Before you seek this type of publicity, make sure you spend some time thinking about what you are going to say. In addition, if you feel you are not a good speaker, you may not want to interview until you have received some training or practice. A poor interview can cause you to lose potential book sales, so do your homework. Every author must learn to speak publicly about your book and sound passionate. If you are apprehensive about public speaking, consider joining local chapters of Toastmasters, a speaking organization for exposure and practice. Community colleges and adult learning centers usually offer speaking courses during the year.

Our company offers a *Career Development Seminar for Motivational Speakers/Authors*. The seminar covers talent/skills assessment, essential elements for speakers, successful marketing strategies, and an open discussion period. If you need specialized training, personal coaching sessions are available. For more information on our seminars or coaching sessions, call U R Gems Group, Inc. at (281) 596-8330.

Make sure you know the name of the radio station and host, what city you are in and mention the radio station and their generosity. You can offer to provide sample interview questions for the host as a professional courtesy. This will help eliminate any unexpected or embarrassing questions. Remember that you want to be asked for a return interview in the future. Do you think the radio station might be offended if you forgot the name of the host? A famous author appeared on a live radio show and asked the host "What city am I in?" She had been on a 12-city tour in two weeks and was very tired. Can you imagine what happened at her book signing? It's not a good idea to forget where you are when promoting your book.

After your interview, always send the host a thank you note. You'll be surprised how many people overlook this common courtesy. Offer several books to give away to the callers to pique interest in your book. We give the host and support staff an autographed copy of our book. Please don't overlook the receptionist, they greet so many people and rarely get any perks for their tremendous professional efforts. Expressions of gratitude for the receptionist and the staff could lead to a great source for referrals. Besides, when callers phone the station, the receptionist will have all your book information to provide them. Remember, never miss an opportunity to sell or publicize your book!

Here are additional tips from Janice Gibson, President of Three G Communications, a public relations and communications firm:

- Set up an 800 number for orders.

- Offer autographed copies for 800 number orders.

- Offer free autographed books to the radio show host to give to the first few callers.

- Plug (mention) your book title during the interview without sounding like an ad.

- Use word pictures or stories to make your point when practical.

- Always give your web site address. If you do not have a web site, get one as soon as possible.

Other practical tips we recommend in your promotion efforts.

- Be sincere and appreciative. Smile and it will reflect in your voice.

- Be sure you stay on track and cover the major points.

- Try to have some other event following the interview and let the host know about it. For example, you can arrange a book signing, workshop, or speech.

- If your interview is away from your home or office, arrive at least 30 minutes early.

- Write down the key points you want to make in case you forgot them.

- Be nice. Do not interrupt the host or take over the interview. Focus on the needs of the radio audience and not just on your desire to sell books.

TV Talk Shows

Television is another excellent source of publicity. However, it requires more preparation. You not only have to be prepared for what you are going to say, but how you appear on the screen. For example, certain colors or types of attire can create the wrong image for you. Do not wear white or stripes. The stations can help you in this area, but make sure you ask. Watch what the news anchors and talk show hosts wear and dress accordingly. Always arrive at least one hour early for makeup preparation and staging set-up such as microphone checks, segment timing,, seating arrangements, and props arrangements.

Whenever speaking publicly, always avoid caffeine drinks, and milk based products (two hours prior to speaking) because they can cause nasal drainage and tickling of the throat. You don't want to clear your throat constantly during a live interview. Some talk shows may have an audience, so practice looking at the audience and smiling. Try to remain relaxed and confident during your interview.

You should start locally and build to nationally televised shows as you gain experience and confidence. Local public and cable stations are a good starting point. Local morning shows are a good source of publicity. As you gain momentum with your television interviews, you may want to seek help from companies that provide national media exposure services. A web site source for guest listing is www.guestfinder.com. This web site offers listings of speakers, experts, authors for television and radio producers to view for possible guests. Another popular source is the *Radio-TV Interview Report*. They send a newsletter to thousands of radio and television producers. You can pay for an ad that features your book and they will help you write the ad.

Be cautious before you go national. Be sure you are prepared to handle the potential demand. For example, it is not unusual to sell thousands of books after an appearance on a nationally syndicated talk show. Everyone knows if your book is merely mentioned on the Oprah Winfrey Show, you probably have a bestseller! Imagine how many lost sales you would experience, if you had not planned in advance for this level of sales through wholesalers, bookstores or order fulfillment services.

If you have budget constraints or lack the time for professional assistance, you can arrange your national television interview entirely yourself. Your library may have *Talk Show Selects*. This book has a listing of the most popular radio and talk shows.

Importance of Media Kits

Many television and talk show producers will want to see your media kit before they invite you on their shows. Media kits should be professional and organized. Media kits are professional design marketing materials for your book. Items to include in the kit are:

✓9 x12 glossy folder	✓business card or book postcard
✓cover letter	✓book summary or book review
✓book cover/jacket	✓newspaper/magazine articles
✓testimonials	✓endorsements
✓news release	✓B&W photograph (or color)
✓your bio	✓an order form for copy of book
✓bookmarks (optional)	✓interview form with questions
✓list previous interviews	✓cassette tape (optional)
✓tour schedule (if available)	✓promotional flyers (optional)

Enclose this information in a high-quality, glossy folder. If possible, glue your front book cover on the outside of the folder. Place your copy or content on your custom letterhead prominently displaying your logo. Be sure to place a label on the back of your photograph that contains your name and contact information. Use your creative ability to make your folder distinctive. Organize the information in your folder in layered format to be easily read. You can also place a portion of this information on your web site in a section for media information.

Distributors

If you are planning to do business with bookstore chains, most will require you to be set up with a distributor or wholesaler. Distributors can be an excellent resource for a self-publisher. A distributor can make your life a lot easier. They sell your book to bookstores, take orders for you, store or warehouse your books, bill the bookstore, collect from the bookstore, ship the book for you, keep track of inventory and finally pay you. Some may provide other marketing services for a fee, such as book cover design and marketing plan assistance. However, their best service is in the area of distribution and sales.

The bad news, this service can cost up to 70% of the price of your book. In other words, if your book sells for $10.00, they will keep $7.00 and send you $3.00. In addition, it can take up to 120 days before you get paid, depending on which distributor you are using. Remember that a distributor has to accept you as a client, but getting one is not always easy. You will also have to give the distributor an exclusive right to sell your books to major bookstore chains. In other words, you cannot have more than one distributor selling your book to the national bookstore market. If your book does not generate enough sales, they will return them to you and charge you a return fee plus freight charge. Distributors are in business to make a profit. You can review the chart in Chapter 3 on distributors and wholesalers differences.

Wholesalers

Wholesalers are similar to distributors, except they don't have a sales force working for you. They will take orders and warehouse your book, but they normally are not actively selling your book. They offer publishers opportunities to promote their titles in their quarterly targeted sales catalogs to bookstores and book readers. Your sales catalogs advertisements should be professionally designed and written to maximize your marketing efforts. Remember that you should always be personally involved with promoting and marketing your book anyway.

The two largest national wholesalers are Ingram and Baker & Taylor. There are also many regional wholesalers. A good resource for wholesalers is *Literary Market Place*. Additionally, some wholesalers are mentioned in the Appendix.

One advantage wholesalers have over distributors is their fee. They usually charge 50-60% of the retail price of your book. If they charge 60% and your book sells for $10.00, they will keep $6.00 of the purchase price and send you $4.00. As with any company, you need to check the company out *before* you sign any agreement. Also, it's a good idea to have your agreement or contract reviewed by a qualified professional before you sign. An attorney who works with authors and publishers is a good resource. You can also seek help through Publishers Marketing Association (PMA) or a local writers' organization that caters to self-publishers.

Libraries

Libraries can be a good source since there are thousands of them in America. However, they are the most skilled and informed potential customers. They will easily recognize a well-written book and a poor quality book too. So, if you are thinking about targeting libraries, do not start until you are sure your book has been well written, edited and is of high quality.

One perceived disadvantage to a library lies with the limited amount of books they will ultimately buy from you. In other words, do not expect a single library to buy large quantities of your books. One bookstore may order ten or more books at a time. A library may order just one or two copies for their branch and may not reorder the book. However, there are nearly 100,000 public, school, college, government, church, and military libraries. Another advantage of selling to libraries is they do not normally return books they purchase. Bookstores must return books if they do not sell, because they are profit driven.

Most libraries will go through a wholesaler to order books. Baker & Taylor caters to this market and will take a 55% or more discount. Baker & Taylor works with all types of publishers. If you want to engage them as a wholesaler, request their Vendor Profile Questionnaire and New Title Information Sheet. Their main phone number is (908) 541-7000. They also have publisher-marketing programs you may choose to use. For more information, visit their web site at www.btol.com.

You may also enter this market by attending library trade shows and conventions, using direct mail ads or using a distributor with special relationships with libraries such as Quality Books. Sometimes libraries will contact the publisher regarding your book after gathering information from your ISBN registration. This happened with our popular inspirational book, *Turning Stones Into Gems*. Apparently, someone had recommended our book to a librarian and they added it to their recommended purchase list.

Bookstores

Independent bookstores are much more likely to take on your book. You may have to offer it on a consignment basis, but what do you have to lose. Of course, you do have to be comfortable that you will be paid when your book sells. We talked about this in an earlier chapter. However, your task will usually be a lot easier getting into a local bookstore than a national chain.

Independent stores usually require a 40% discount. They often pay quicker than wholesalers who may take up to four months to pay you. Some distributors will let you deal with local bookstores even though you have signed an exclusive agreement with them. They may do this because they would rather work with the major bookstore chains.

Major bookstores will usually order their books through wholesalers and distributors. This makes economic sense because they only have to invoice a few wholesalers versus hundreds or thousands of authors and publishers.

If enough people come to a bookstore to buy your book, an aggressive bookstore will order your book. Bookstores want to track continual sales of your book, not just selling books when you are in the store. If this trend continues, it may open the door for you to get your book on the shelf. However, if you are not constantly promoting your book, this may be a short-lived accomplishment and your book will be returned.

Don't get angry with the bookstore if they return your books after you sell 40-50 books during your book signing. What happens after your event is more important to them. You have to sell books all the time! Always ask your readers to recommend their friends to come back and purchase your book. Autograph extra books for the store when you leave. Think of ways to bring people back to the store to buy your book is very important. You can write articles for a community newspaper, newsletters, speaking events, participate in fundraisers, etc.

Nonprofit Organizations

Charitable and other nonprofit organizations constantly need to raise money for their causes. Most sell products or have fundraising events to finance their programs. Contact some of these organizations that are compatible with the subject matter of your book. For example, if your book is on drug abuse, you could contact one of the organizations that sponsors drug abuse programs.

A good source for finding associations is the *Encyclopedia of Associations*. Your local library should have a copy of this resource book in the reference section. You can search on the Internet using key words. For example, typing in the words "drug abuse associations" will produce a list of potential customers. When you find a good prospect to purchase your books, offer them a 20%-50% discount, depending on how many books they purchase.

Specialty Shops

New authors often overlook specialty shops as a source to sell their books. For example, a gardening book could be sold at a hardware store or nursery. A fishing book could be sold at a bait and tackle shop or sporting goods store. First, start with independent shops, because it is easier to get to the decision maker. Getting your book in a chain store will be more difficult. You may have to go to their wholesaler or distributor. Ask the store manager who supplies them their books. They are usually very helpful.

If the store does not carry books, you have to convince them why selling books will benefit the store. Another option is to go to one of the store's wholesalers or sales representatives and pitch them to sell your books. If they agree, you must pay them a percentage of net sales and give the store a 40-50% or more discount on your books. If you have priced your books correctly, you should still be able to make a profit. Chains usually order more books, sometimes thousands at a time. The prospect of selling thousands of books to one customer is well worth the effort.

Internet

The potential of the Internet is enormous. Amazon.com online bookstore has over 1,000,000 titles on its web site. A major advantage of marketing on the Internet is the lower cost of this media compared to print media, radio or television. You can also update your site daily, weekly, or monthly very inexpensively. The appearance of your site can position you to be much more established than you really are. A professional looking web site gives perceived credibility to many potential buyers.

Many online bookstores will consider selling your books on their web sites. Two of the largest are Amazon.com and Barnes&Noble.com. Other sites that cater specifically to the book market are listed below. However, you can design and publish your own site with the use of software such as Microsoft® FrontPage®, Adobe® PageMill®, Macromedia® Dreamweaver™, etc. However, a professionally designed web site requires months of training or practice. The time you spend on this may be better used writing, promoting, and selling books.

Addresses for sites are:

Amazon: www.amazon.com

Barnes & Noble: www.bn.com

Borders: www.borders.com

cushcity.com: www.cushcity.com

mosaicbooks.com www.mosaicbooks.com

Book Clubs

Book clubs do not usually offer you much money for your book. Your book will probably be sold at a 20%-30% discount off regular retail price. A royalty of 5%-10% will normally be paid from book sales. However, book clubs may offer a large degree of exposure and credibility to your book. You can use this when you are marketing your book to libraries, wholesalers, distributors, etc. Also, many book clubs will buy large volumes of books directly from the publisher. This practice will permit you to print more books and take advantage of volume discounts from your printer. In other words, you can reduce the cost of each book and increase the profit you earn from each book. Smaller book clubs may simply want a 60%-80% discount on your book.

A list of book clubs can be found in our Resource Guides and the *Literary Market Place*. You should think carefully about this outlet. Some publishers go to book clubs when they think their book sales have declined to a low point. The small royalty the club pays may be better than the publisher could get otherwise. However, established book clubs can offer prestige and credibility for your book as well as boost sales. Often, book club purchases do not conflict with other markets for your book. In other words, certain people use book clubs for most of their book purchases. They would not normally go to the bookstore or online to shop for a book.

Direct Mail Order

The direct mail order business is a multi-billion dollar industry. Books are no exception, especially *how to* or informational books.

Although many mail-order books are ordered through book clubs or online bookstores such as Amazon.com and Barnes&Noble.com, you can also put together your own marketing campaign. Classified ads in newspapers or magazines are sources you may consider. Also, *renting* mailing lists from list brokers, magazines, or other sources is another way to target retailers, independent bookstores, libraries and consumers. However, you should pursue free publicity and advertising before you spend much of your money on direct mail. If you do use direct mail, make sure you are getting directly to the people or companies that you want to buy your book. Using targeted mailing lists will help reach your target buyer, but you should try to use a list broker that is reputable and whose lists are effective.

Try asking other authors, trade associations, and publishers for recommendations. You can also visit www.literarymarketplace.com to get names of some mailing list brokers and services.

The *American Book Trade Directory* is an inexpensive source for bookstores. From this source, you can find the names, addresses, and phone numbers of bookstores in America and Canada. *The American Library Directory* is a source for locating library addresses. It provides a list of most of the libraries in the United States and Canada. Both of these reference books can be found in local libraries.

Other organizations such as the American Booksellers Association, *Publishers Marketing Association and Gale Research Company* may be approached for mailing lists. Fees for renting lists range from $45.00 to more than $100.00 per thousand names. Lists can be customized to fit the target audience you are seeking.

Testing Direct Mail Ads

Testing is especially valuable in the mail-order industry. Before you spend your entire direct mail budget on an ad, you might want to have a trial run. For example, instead of sending out 1,000 letters or post cards on one ad you might send out only 300. Or you might send out 500 cards with one ad and 500 cards with a different ad.

One ad may have significantly more response than the other. You will then know to go with the ad that received the better response. Later, you may want to test prices to see whether one price gets a significantly better response. Sometimes a higher price gets more orders than a lower price. The main point is that you need to start out small before you spend money unnecessarily. Once you know you have a proven winning ad, then you can spend money wisely. Although testing is a useful technique, timing issues may restrict the use of this tool. You must decide which titles or products are best feasible to test.

Keying Ads

Keying ads simply means coding a mailing in a way that you can tell which ad an order came from and how many orders came from a particular ad. The importance of this is obvious. You don't want to spend your money on an ad or source that does not earn you enough money to profit from the ad.

Examples of different ways to key an ad are as follows:

◆ You can add "Dept. X" in your return mailing address. Different sources will have different department numbers. For example, Dept. PA could be the code for Parents Magazine.

◆ You could use different toll-free numbers to identify an ad or source of an ad. Let's say you wanted to run two different ads in the same newspaper. You could use an 800 number for the ad in the business section and an 888 number for the ad in the sports section.

◆ A combination letter, numbering system could be used. The letter identifies the publication and the number identifies the particular issue of the publication. For example, PM-6 could be used in the address as Dept. PM-6. This would tell you the order or inquiry came from the June (sixth month) issue of Parents Magazine (PM).

◆ You can simply require customers to use a code number when responding to the ad.

◆ You can offer a free report, booklet, etc. in your ad and assign a number that will identify the publication or ad.

Importance of the Headline

Headlines sell ads. You often have only a few seconds to grab the addition of a reader. The headline is the vehicle that makes or breaks your ad. There are professional copywriters that can write ads for you. However, if you are dealing with a limited budget, you may be able to do this yourself. Classified ads are a popular and relatively inexpensive way to start advertising your book. Certain key words in ads have been used time and time again. The reason you see them so often is because they have proven to work for many ads. There is no guarantee they will work in every ad you write, but your odds of getting the attention should improve when you do use them.

A few of the attention-getting words and phrases are:

◆ Free	◆ New	◆ Introducing
◆ Proven	◆ Finally	◆ Announcing
◆ How to	◆ Now	◆ At last
◆ Why	◆ Learn	◆ Amazing

Other Things You May Consider Including In An Ad

◆ **Testimonials**—people want to know what others think about your book.

◆ **Free Offer**—if you say free, it must be free. Even if they return your book, they keep the gift.

◆   **Endorsements**—help to establish credibility.

◆   **Guarantee**—you may want to test this before you go full scale, but guarantees have been proven to work. Many consumers won't buy mail-order products without a guarantee.

Examples of Headlines

Announcing A New, Revolutionary Way to Publish Books
Finally. . .A Proven News Release That Works!
Publish Your Book in One Day...Guaranteed
How To Write A Book in 30 Days

Exercise Caution

There are important federal laws regarding mail-order business. Before you start using this type of distribution outlet, you should send to the Federal Trade Commission, Washington, DC 20580 or call (202) 326-2222 for information on mail-order regulations.

Book Signings

Book signings are great, especially when you see your name on the posters in the front of the store. However, book signings can be very disappointing if you don't publicize the event in advance to the right audience. You can get all dressed up for your party and no one shows up! Most local bookstores are usually willing to work with you on book signings. The reason they have book signings is to sell books! You must be able to bring customers in the store consistently to buy your books. Always think of ways to keep your customers buying your book.

Ask if the bookstores have mailing lists and can announce your event in advance to their customers. Discuss if they will announce your signing in their newsletters, mailers, flyers, etc. Allow enough lead-time before confirming your signing date. Beware of last minute fill-in signings, because you may not have adequate time to publicize the event. If you don't let people know you are having a party, why have it? Send out personal announcements to your contacts as well. Inquire about contacting local book and reading clubs; some may even meet in the bookstore. Try contacting them and coincide your signing and discussion with a book club meeting. Send news releases to newspapers, radio stations, television stations, and organizations that would announce or post your event. Send your own release even if the bookstore sends one.

Always arrive at least 30-45 minutes before your event to ensure everything is set up properly. If you expect a large crowd (more than 20 people), bring a microphone. Most bookstores will not supply microphones. An inexpensive suggestion, use a karaoke machine with medium speakers and a wireless microphone. Ask the store personnel to announce your signing several times before your event and several times during your event. Write your own announcement, keep it brief, and always mention benefits of attending your event. People love giveaways, drawings, and free stuff!

You may want to pre-sign books to expedite the process. However, be sure you ask the buyers for their names to complete. Plan on decorating your table with balloons, signs, and posters to attract attention. Author, Pat G'Orge-Walker, and creator of *shameless promotions*, suggests setting up your table near the bestsellers or nationally known recommended reading lists or clubs. You can increase the traffic to your area and always try to compare your book to a similar best-seller or mention your book will be there one day! Always ask attendants for their names on your mailing list to offer future announcements, events, books, newsletters, contests, giveaways, thank-you cards, etc.

Seminars

Seminars are excellent ways to add value to a book signing. People are more likely to buy your book after you have given them useful information. Our company gives seminars for Aspiring Writers, Motivational Speakers/Trainers and on Career Development. Details on our seminars can be found in our corporate web site at www.urgems.com or in our author web site at www.sarafreemansmith.com. From time to time, U R Gems Group offers *free* mini-seminars at selected bookstores. We are able to combine the seminar and book signing into one event. The response is excellent because we do more than simply market our books.

Other Successful Ideas for Book Promotion

Many new authors face challenges of attracting people to their book signing events especially at crowded venues like bookstores, conventions, and conferences. One author solved that problem by purchasing a bubble-blowing gadget. Visit a toy store for novelty ideas such as Santa, teddy bears, dolls, etc. The bubbles attracted children and their parents to her table. She told the curious visitors that her book had great tips to float away their stress just like the bubbles. This would be a great idea for a children's book, weight reduction, etc.

Buy an autograph book or wedding reception registry book to have your book buyers and attendees sign for you. Explain you want to send them a thank you note, add them to your mailing list for future announcements, newsletters, or upcoming books. It's a great way to express your gratitude and it helps you remember their names when you are signing. The book will always be organized for updating to a database for e-mail or snail mail (regular mailing).

In addition to sending thank you notes to bookstores, book clubs, radio, or television stations, send them a certificate of appreciation. Most software programs have certificate templates that can be customized. Thank the organization (by name) for their kind support of your book (complete book title), sign it, and frame it. Deliver the certificate personally unless they are located out of town. Hopefully, the staff and potential buyers will see it displayed. The publicity and exposure is immeasurable and it will help develop a solid relationship with your supporters.

"The talent of success is nothing more than doing what you can do well, and doing well whatever you do!"

—Henry Longfellow

Chapter 8

Developing A Marketing Plan

"Often times, your plans fail because you fail to plan."

Why You Need A Plan

Suppose you have to drive to a city for the first time. Your destination is 800 miles away and you are not exactly sure how to get there. You know you have to go west on I-10 until you get to San Antonio, but you don't have a clue which freeways you have to take next. What do you do? If you are like most people, you get a map or you call the auto club and ask them to mark the route for you on a map. You want to know the fastest, safest way to get to your destination. Can you imagine going on an extended trip not knowing exactly how to get there? Well, that's exactly what you would be doing if you published your book without a marketing plan. A marketing plan is your road map to guide you on your journey to a successful book. It should be completed *before* your book is published.

In an earlier chapter, we mentioned another reason to have a marketing plan. If you are planning to market your book in bookstores or libraries, most wholesalers and distributors will want to see that you have one. They want to know you have given serious thought about how your book will be sold. They also want to see if your plan makes sound business sense. Remember, self-publishing is a business and no reputable wholesaler or distributor wants to waste their time with an author that is not committed to making his or her book successful. So take the time or have some of the free resources help you develop a plan in writing. Organizations such as the Small Business Administration, SCORE and various other government-sponsored economic development centers can probably help you with your marketing plan. We also develop marketing plans for new authors or you may seek assistance from PMA.

Getting Started

We will focus on six areas in developing your marketing plan, namely:

1. Target Audience—Who will buy your book? Why?

2. Market Strategy, Position & Theme

3. Sales & Promotional Tools

4. Budget

5. Distribution Channels

6. Book Production Schedule

Target Audience

The first thing you should ask yourself is why would someone want to buy your book? "Because I *need* the money is *not* a good answer." People must have a good reason to buy your book *before* they spend their money. In other words, what's in it for them?

Before you spend money on printing your books, you had better have a good answer for this question.

Other questions you should answer are:

1. What benefits will my book offer?

2. Who is most likely to benefit from your book?

3. Who will find my book valuable, interesting, or informative?

4. Why did I or why will I write the book?

5. Can I narrow my market to a select group of readers?

6. How do I get to the people I want to buy my book?

7. How large is my target audience?

8. How much will people pay for my book?

9. What is unique about my book?

10. What other books are similar to yours? What's your competition?

Initially, you probably will not be able to answer all of the above questions. However, you must attempt to answer most of them. If you don't, you are probably going to be less effective than someone who can answer these questions. You will be driving in the dark with no lights on your journey to a successful book. Maybe you will still reach your destination. However, the odds are against you though. You won't know to whom you are selling, why they would buy your book, how many people would buy it or, how to get to them.

Let's say you did your homework. You researched in the library. You read trade magazines, you asked the librarian for help, and you asked your friends. You were able to learn a lot about your target audience and book. Your research revealed that there were more than 50,000 family abuse victims each year in your hometown alone that could benefit from your book. Similar books were written on your topic that retailed for between $10.00-$15.00. People of varying financial and ethnic backgrounds were in your target market. Finally, you realized you wrote the book because you grew up in a dysfunctional family and successfully survived the ordeal. Your book not only contained your personal testimony, but also offered considerably more resources than the other books.

Market Strategy

Here's just a sample of what you can do with this information:

1. You can go to the *Encyclopedia of Associations* in the library and get the names of organizations that serve family abuse victims. You can offer to speak to these organizations and support groups. You can offer your book as a resource after you speak. You can hand out a mailing list at the beginning of your speech. You can plan for a future newsletter. The newsletter will market other products and services you plan to sell later.

2. You want people to know how to get out of this situation or how to put their lives back together. You can write an article on the subject and send it to several women's magazines. You also may *rent* a mailing list from those magazines to use in a direct mail campaign. Magazines will lend or rent you a list of their subscribers for a fee.

3. You can launch a web site for family abuse victims. The web site includes a chat room where victims could e-mail under assumed names to discuss different issues. You can include links to other organizations from which they can seek for help. Excerpts from your book may be included on your site, along with ordering information. The site may include a credit card secure server for ordering online.

Are you starting to get the picture? You can accomplish a great deal with the right information. However, without a clear focus, you are not going to be as effective.

Let's personalize this information for your book. Take a piece of paper and describe your book in one or two sentences. Now list the features of your book and what makes it unique or better than similar books. For example, your book has more pages, has personal stories, gives more resource material, etc. Next, list the advantages of buying your book, such as: inspiration, motivation, entertainment, informs or helps improve the reader's life. Now describe your target audience by listing all the people that will want and need your book. Consider sex, age, marital status, income, race, education, memberships, hobbies, entertainment interests, reading preferences, radio station interests, etc. Now consider organizations and companies that will want your book.

Position & Theme

Because you now know whom your audience is and how to find them, you now need your hook. You have to capture them and confirm them to loyal customers. Remember, you came from a dysfunctional family, you know first hand how to survive it. You know so much about the subject matter, you wrote a book to help others. Because you have written a book, you are now considered an expert.

Now that you are an expert, you position yourself as the expert on family abuse. Using some of the tools mentioned in Chapter 7 and below, you start discussing the problem on radio and television talk shows. You conduct mini-seminars at bookstores and autograph books for your audience. You moderate forums for victims of family abuse on your web site. You offer to speak at various events, meetings, and church functions and sell your books when you finish. You write articles in magazines, newspapers, newsletters, etc. You have now positioned yourself as an expert. People will buy your book because the information will benefit them.

Up to now, we have used a hypothetical book project. In this step, you are going to think of ways your actual book can get the attention of your target audience. This may be the book cover, the title, the price of your book compared to similar books, the image you want to convey, the unique market you are trying to target, a theme that complement your book, the unique benefit your book offers, the added value you offer, the way you are going to capture your audience, etc. Anything that you feel makes your book unique from a sales standpoint should be listed here. For example, if you feel all the books on your subject are too technical, write a book that is easy to understand. If you know all the books on your subject are too simple, write one that is technical.

Making your book unique will often require you to target a different market, even though the subject matter may be the same. A technical book may be better for the professional market. A simple, easily understood book may be better for children or the mass consumer market.

Sales & Promotional Tools

You need to choose the tools you are going to use to get to your audience. You can reach them many ways. Several are mentioned below:

◆News Releases	◆Word of Mouth
◆Radio Talk Shows	◆Television Talk Shows
◆Seminars	◆Book Signings
◆Flyers	◆Feature Articles
◆T-shirts	◆Endorsements /Reviews
◆Public Speaking	◆Fund Raisers
◆Sponsorships	◆Newsletters
◆Trade Shows	◆Gift Certificates
◆Business Cards	◆Newspaper Classified Ads
◆Logos	◆Magazine Classified Ads

You need to decide what makes good sense for you. Some of these items involve spending money, so you need to spend some time with weighing the rewards versus the expense. When starting out, you should spend as little money as possible. Therefore, whenever possible, take advantage of publicity and other low cost tools.

When we were creating the marketing plan for *Turning Stones Into Gems,* one of the tools we decided to use was the seminar. Sara had a substantial amount of experience in career development. The seminars provided a way to get to our target audience as well as pass on the benefit of her experience. At the same time, we could offer an autographed copy of her book at the end of the seminar. We gave our audience *valuable, free* information as added value. We had positioned ourselves uniquely from other authors using these two tools.

Distribution Channels

Now you must decide how you are going to get your books to your audience. We went through an exercise in Chapter 3 to help you determine your profit margin, or how much you could earn from your book after expenses. Now you need to choose the different channels of distribution you will use in selling your book. Base your selections on your results from that analysis.

As a reminder, some of the channels are wholesalers, distributors, bookstores, libraries, retail stores, Internet, mail order, book clubs, etc. Once you have selected your channels of distribution, you are ready to determine your budget.

Budget

Use the chart provided at the end of the chapter to record the tools you want and how much they will cost. If you are like most new authors, you will not have a lot to spend on advertising and promotion. Unless you have money you are willing to lose, we would gradually increase spending as exposure and interest in your book increases. However, take advantage of as much free publicity as possible before you spend much money on promotion. Keep advertising to a minimum unless you have a large budget. Much of your advertising should be targeted to your specific audience. This can be done through mailing lists you accumulate or rent from list brokers, magazines, and other sources that know how to get to your audience. Avoid spending large sums of your budget on display ads in magazines, unless you are certain you will get enough orders to pay for your ad and earn a reasonable profit. Authors often do not recover their costs in such ads because hundreds or thousands of book orders must be realized to cover the cost of advertising.

Book Production Schedule

Timing is often a critical element in avoiding unnecessary delays in producing a book. Begin now to develop a timeline for completing projects with your book. For example, you need to obtain certain information before you can finish a cover design. The cover design can take as much as three months to complete. If you wait until you are almost ready to send your book to the printer, you may find yourself three months behind schedule. Certain registrations take several weeks, if you don't apply for them ahead of time, you may be further delayed.

You must understand the importance of planning and maintaining a schedule. A sample book production schedule is provided in the Appendix.

Budget Planner

TOOL	COST/UNIT	MONTHLY USE	MONTHLY COST
		Grand Total	

Chapter 9

Tips & Resources for Women and Minorities

"You don't write because you want to say something, you write because you've got something to say."
F. Scott Fitzgerald

For one thing, an author may go to a vanity publisher who is more concerned about the fee than the quality of the work. In another case, an author may take his or her book to a *printer* who does not specialize in *book printing*. A book printer may not have the best equipment for the type of book design or X you desire. Many book designs really require a professional book designer instead of a relative or friend who is cheaper. In many of these cases, the net result could be a book that looks like it was thrown together in a day.

Over the years, these types of poor quality products have closed doors for many self-published authors. However, although we faced some of the same obstacles, we were able to overcome them. How did we do this? We didn't listen to all the reasons why we should not self-publish and focused on why we should. In doing so, we completed our book and, during the process, identified several myths about self-publishing.

Six Myths About Self-Published Authors

1. Minorities do not buy books

Every successful minority author can laugh all the way to the bank on this one! Can you imagine where Iyanla Vanzant, Toni Morrison, Terry McMillan, E. Lynn Harris, Eric Jerome Dickey, Amy Tan would be if not for the purchasing power of their avid minority fans? The mainstream publishing industry has perpetuated this myth for many years but the statistics are untrue. Beginning in the early 90's, the publishing industry began to take notice of successful books written by minorities such as Terry McMillan (*Waiting to Exhale*), Walter Mosley (*Devil with the Blue Dress*) and Amy Tan (*The Joy Luck Club*).

The success of those authors and others has caused the publishing houses to develop specialty imprints (divisions) to focus on a market that existed all along. Minorities will buy books for the same reasons other consumers buy them: entertainment, information, or inspiration. Looking at the commercial success of such books as *Roots, The Color Purple, Waiting to Exhale* and *Devil in the Blue Dress* can easily destroy that myth. These books were successfully adapted for television and film.

There are literally thousands of minority book club members throughout the country that get together to discuss new books they purchased. Visit a national bookstore and observe the obvious ethnic diversity throughout bookstore. Something not so obvious is the increasing number of minorities ordering online and through mail order. Also, don't forget many books are sold at conventions and conferences. Such sales are hard to track, but we know from personal experience, minorities buy books at conventions.

2. Self-published authors are not credible

Did you know the books listed below were all self-published? Major publishing firms currently publish these successful best-selling authors. Their successful marketing and sales efforts caught the attention of the national publishers. Ask their loyal readers if their credibility was ever in question!

Invisible Life by E. Lynn Harris
What Color is Your Parachute? by Richard Bolles
The One Minute Manager by Ken Blanchard & Spencer Johnson
The Christmas Box by Rick Evans
In Search of Excellence by Tom Peters
The Celestine Prophesy by James Redfield
Woman, Thou Art Loosed by T.D. Jakes
Brothers, Lust and Love by William July II
Emily, The Yellow Rose by Anita Richmond Bunkley
Behind Closed Doors by Kimberla Lawson Roby
Three Perfect Men, The Price of Passion, Dangerous Dilemmas by
                    Evelyn Palfrey

3. Lack of exposure

New authors expect immediate recognition and exposure because they have a book—so what? Remember, it's not important to people that you have a book, what's important are the benefits your book will provide them. You need exposure for your book but focus on the benefits and features of your book.

Lack of exposure from the media may have been a valid concern at one time, but technology has leveled the playing field. Fax or e-mail a powerful news release and watch the resulting publicity generate book sales. Promote your book via an online bookstore and tell people to order your books from the online bookstore. Authors can tap into the awesome power of publicity by appearing on talk radio or television shows. Many of these shows don't care if your books are self-published as long as you have something they feel will benefit their audience.

4. Major bookstores are not interested in self-published authors

You would not be reading this book without the overwhelming support we initially received from the major and independent bookstores in Houston, Texas.

All bookstores want to sell books regardless who published them. Likewise, chain bookstores are interested in supporting their local authors because people will support and buy their books. They often do this through maintaining contact with leaders of the local writers' organizations. At least once a year, chain bookstores will invite local organizations to participate in an event. There's a little catch though; you have to join and be active in one of the writers' groups. Go to a chain store and find out which local groups they support or invite to their special events. Then contact them and attend their next meeting. Join at least one that has members who are self-published authors and get involved with their activities. You will be able to get advice from other authors and stay current with issues and trends that affect the publishing business.

There's one other major obstacle if you want your book in a chain bookstore. You need a wholesaler or distributor Bookstores want to have a single ordering source. This was explained in Chapter 7. Chain bookstores do not want to receive invoices from hundreds or thousands of different authors. Therefore, they order from wholesalers or distributors. You must apply to one of these companies to have your book(s) added to their warehouse inventory.

The largest wholesalers in the country are Ingram and Baker & Taylor. They have started special programs for small publishers, such as Ingram Express, which makes it easier for small publishers to be accepted. More information on Ingram and Baker & Taylor is located in the Appendix.

Bookstore chains also want your book to look like a good investment to the reader. The importance of a good book design and book layout plays a major factor, too. In the past, many authors used vanity publishers and were not accepted by major chains due to poor book quality. Some chains will not accept books from certain vanity publishers regardless of the subject.

5. It's too expensive

Technology is continuing to open new doors for self-published authors. For example, *print-on-demand, e-books,* and other technology make it possible to print your book in very small quantities. These new technologies will be discussed in more detail later in this chapter. For example, DocuTech® equipment developed by Xerox® can be used to print a perfect-bound book in runs of 50 books or less. You can test the demand for your book for as little as $100.

Our first edition of *Turning Stones Into Gems* was printed for less than $200. We used plastic comb binding instead of perfect binding and sold the books at a convention. We continued to do this at small bookstores, church events, special book signing events, etc. Using part of our earnings from the first edition, we used a book printer to produce our second edition in perfect-bound form. We were then ready to get our book on the shelf in major chains in our local area. They were very receptive because they already knew there was a demand for the book. With technology now available, you can now test with actual perfect bound books and e-books instead of using plastic comb binding.

Even though bookstores may not be willing to put your book on their shelf, many will special order your book if a customer wants it. However, you must have your book listed in *Books in Print*, which requires you to have an ISBN. This number was explained in Chapter Five. Keep in mind though you have more ways to sell your book than in bookstores. Chapter 7 gives more detail on how and where you can sell books. Be creative and try to think of new ways to sell your books. You are your own boss now. Don't be afraid to test non-traditional methods. Many entrepreneurs have become millionaires by trying new ways of doing things. They were no different from most of us. They had an idea, and they put it into action.

6. Self-Published books have poor packaging and layout

In many cases, this may be true. However, it does not have to be the case. Affordable word processing and book formatting software such as Corel WordPerfect®, MicrosoftWord®, PageMaker®, and QuarkXPress® all make this a myth. Some vanity publishers and printers may produce a book that looks like it was published in your garage. That's why you have to be very careful whom you choose to print your book. Ask for samples of their work before you decide. Make sure you are dealing with a *book* printer. This type of printer specializes in printing books and has the right type of equipment to produce a high quality book. Also, ask other authors about a company before you make your final decision. If a company is terrible, other authors will remember its name and advise you against it.

Many book printers now have templates you can use for your book cover design. We recommend you hire a graphic artist that specializes in designing book covers. Some of them are very expensive, charging $1,500 to $3,000 to do your cover. We have found there are artists who do this part time that are just as good as the cover design companies. Ask your local writers' groups for names. Many of them have a small network of people they work with that can help you.

What about finances?

Dealing with a tight budget

If you are like most of us, your book budget is tight. We do not advocate betting the farm to publish your book. Earlier we mentioned that we published our first book, *Turning Stones Into Gems* for less than $300. We were comfortable risking this amount on our project. You know what works for you. Keep part of your profits from your first book run to produce more books in your second printing. Remember, your cost per book declines as you print larger quantities of books. For example, 500 copies of a 96-page book might cost $2.00 per copy or $1,000. Increase the printing to

2,500 books and the cost drops to $0.70 per copy or $1,750. You ordered five times more books, but paid less than twice as much. Here again, use good judgment. As demand for your book increases, then you know to print larger quantities. However, if sales are going very slowly, why print a five-year supply of books? Your focus in this instance would be more on how to speed up sales instead of how much you can save on printing costs.

Remember that it's possible to pre-sell books before you actually have them printed. For example, if you are selling books as premiums or company giveaways, you can ask for a deposit or down payment on the order before you deliver. If you have priced your books correctly, the initial down payment will cover most or all of your printing costs.

Print-on-Demand

New technology available today means great news for minorities and women. We are focusing on these groups, because we are the ones who traditionally have more problems financing our book projects. On-demand digital printing allows you to have your book printed in very small quantities on an *as needed* basis. Therefore, you can produce a high quality book at a fraction of the cost of traditional printing. Although your cost per book will be higher, your risks of printing books that do not sell are substantially reduced. You only have to order when you get orders for your book. Also, there are now companies that will print your book for as little as $100 and pay you a royalty of 20% to 50%. Such companies should not be confused with traditional vanity publishers. These are high quality books and some of the companies can arrange for your books to be made available in bookstores. Books can be printed in less than 48 hours. Some of these companies are listed in Chapter 10.

E-Books

Electronic book publishing is another relatively inexpensive way authors can produce book titles. You can offer your book in several electronic formats. Formats such as PDF, HTML, ASCII, XML, and OEB are becoming common. Companies are rapidly entering this relatively new market. Reader appliances and software such as Microsoft Reader®, Palm Pilot®, EB Journal, Gemstar eBook and GlassBook® are gaining momentum. Such products can store several books, eliminating the need to carry heavy or bulky books when you travel. Microsoft, Barnes and Noble, Borders Group, Random House and Simon & Schuster are also joining the race. E-books are discussed in more detail in Chapter 10.

Smaller e-book web sites are popping up offering authors the opportunity to sell their books at a fraction of the cost of traditionally printed books. You can use this new media to test the demand for your book before you spend thousands of dollars printing books.

Co-publishing

Authors who want a financial or experienced partner, more control, or more profits may decide to co-publish. For example, an aspiring author may have a book idea, but does not have enough money or experience to publish it. A small press or experienced author may agree to finance the book's production, provided the aspiring author agrees to perform other duties. The two parties agree in writing on their mutual responsibilities and how the profits will be divided. Ideally, the aspiring author promotes the book and shares in part of the financial risk.

Co-publishing is not the same as vanity publishing. A publisher willing to co-publish does so because they believe they can earn a profit. They are not charging the author a fee to publish the book. In fact, they are assuming part or all of the financial risks involved in publishing and promoting the book. The Spencer Johnson Company and G.P. Putnam co-published *Who Moved My Cheese?* in 1998.

Today, there are over 1.2 million hardcover copies of this bestseller in print. Obviously, co-publishing can be a profitable alternative for many writers.

This publishing option is becoming more popular, but is not easy to secure. You will have to convince someone you are worth the risk. The risks for the financier can be high if all parties involved are not totally committed to the project. Fortunately, there are other options for you to consider, such as e-books, print-on-demand, or small print runs.

Grants, Awards, and Contests

Grants, awards, and contests are another way writers may finance their book projects. Many foundations give writing or publishing grants to organizations or individuals who meet their guidelines. Often, writing awards have cash components that can be used to publish a book. Some writing contests finance the publishing of a book as the grand prize. If you can link a book to the mission of a foundation, they may be willing to pay the costs to print the book. All of these options require much effort on your part. However, the potential payoff is you get your book published free. A partial list of organizations that offer grants, awards, or contests is listed in the Appendix. Other sources may be found through Internet search engines using keywords, such as writing grants, writing contest, or writing awards. The *Literary Market Place* is also a resource available in the reference section of your local library or online at www.literarymarketplace.com.

Credit Cards

Most printers will accept credit cards for payment. Again, use good judgment when charging for purchases. If you cannot pay it back without depending solely on book sales, you are asking for trouble. For one thing, wholesalers can take up to 120 days to pay you after a bookstore buys your books. We have heard of cases where authors never were paid by independent bookstores. When you sell your books without being paid cash on delivery, you take the risk that you won't get paid. So if book sales are the only way you can pay your credit card debt back, you should at least have set aside the first four months of credit card payments. When you get your check from the wholesaler or distributor, you can make major reductions on your credit card balance.

You can't take the Internet lightly

If you are serious about publishing, you need to own a computer and get online. The money you can save by producing your own material will eventually pay for the computer. Also, there is a wealth of information on the Internet you can use in your research. By using search engines, you can find information on virtually any topic. From a marketing standpoint, you must have an Internet presence to maintain a professional image. You don't have to develop your own site right away. When you are ready to have your own site, go to www.writershelpdesk.com for a list of web site designers. PageTurner.net designed our first author site. They specialize in designing sites for authors. Their web site address is www.pageturner.net. You can get started by getting your books on some of the online bookseller web sites, such Amazon.com, Barnes&Noble.com or Borders.com.

You are not alone

Chances are you are going to experience some obstacles you did not anticipate. Be prepared to lose some friends or discover some of your *friends* were not really friends. When you tell your friends, spouse, and relatives, don't be surprised if all of them are not as excited about the project as you. When you have your first book signing, don't expect all of them to come. Some may try to discourage you from completing the book at all. There are a number of reasons for this. It will range from fear of losing you as a friend to just plain jealousy. If it happens to you, don't let anyone stop you from realizing your dream. If you do, you will probably regret it later.

One of our friends is a mortgage banker. She had helped a customer to get her first house. This person had been renting for years, but dreamed of owning her own home. She had saved some money, but was short on the down payment. Our friend made her aware of a special program that provided the rest of the down payment needed to buy a brand new house. Her customer was very excited and shared the good news with her friends who did not own homes either. The day before her customer was scheduled to close, she called and informed our friend she had changed her mind. She went on to explain that her friends had caused her to have second thoughts about buying the house. Real estate prices have increased substantially since then, placing that dream home further out of reach.

What's the point of this story? If this happens to you, you may need to find new friends. Go to our web site and read some of our motivational material. Surround yourself with friends who want to help you. Stay away from the ones who only want to discourage you. Network with other writers in your area. Paste positive phrases or affirmations on your refrigerator, mirrors, in your car, bedroom, etc. Seek spiritual guidance and pray for blessings. Go to the resource section immediately following this chapter and in the Appendix. Do everything you can think of to keep yourself motivated and focused. Do all these things and you will find the strength to overcome the obstacles you will face on the road to a successful book project. We know you can do it!

Resources

Book Consultants

U R Gems Group, Inc.
Mack E. Smith & Sara Freeman Smith
(281) 596-8330
www.urgems.com

Book Cover Designers
(Other book cover designers listed on www.writershelpdesk.com)

Juanita Cole Howard
www.PageTurner.net/Juanita
E-mail: jhowardart@aol.com

Gladys Ramirez (she designed our books)
(713) 228-2495
E-mail:gladysramirez@earthlink.net

Marc Newsome, Volume Media, Inc.
(713) 781-4650
www.volumemediainc.com

Mary Valle-Cooper, Yorké Design
281-485-7138 (voice & fax)
E-mail:yorkedesign@ev1.net.

Book Editors
(Other book editors listed on www.writershelpdesk.com)

Chandra Sparks Taylor
She has worked with some best-selling and established authors and many emerging authors. She does line editing, copyediting, and proofreading for a number of publishers. (718) 341-3688

E-mail: cstedit1@aol.com or curtshamjam@aol.com

Judy King
Judy King Editorial Services: Expert editing, writing, indexing, proofreading. Voice: 713-721-3003; Fax: 713-721-7272; E-mail: judyking@pdq.net.

Melanie Malinowsky, PhD
Works with many emerging and established authors with editing, proofreading, and copyediting needs.
Email:MMalinowsk@aol.com.

Sonya Vann (she edited our second edition)
Email:sonyavann@yahoo.com

Book Packagers

Rita Mills
A book packager working specifically with nonprofits to produce books for fundraising and outreach. A consultant for Asian book printers. E-mail: rmills@ghgcorp.com
www.millsmorrispublishing.com

Distribution
Wholesalers

Wholesalers assists publishers by stocking their books in warehouses and taking orders from bookstores, libraries, etc. They require a 50%-60% discount off the retail price of your book. Additional wholesalers are located in the Appendix at the back of this book.

Ingram Book Company
Public Relations Department
One Ingram Boulevard
LaVergne, TN 37086-3629
Web site: www.ingrambookgroup.com

Ingram is the largest supplier of books to the bookstores and retailers. It has a special program called Ingram Express, which is for publishers who have less than 10 titles. Go to their web site at www.ingrambookgroup.com/Pub_Info/newpubinfo/express.htm on their web site to download the forms and get more information. Ingram has a multi-cultural representative that works with bookstores.

Baker & Taylor Publisher Services
44 Kirby Avenue
Somerville, NJ 08876
Attn: Robin Bright (908) 218-3803
Web site: www.btol.com

Baker & Taylor is a major supplier of books, videotapes, audiotapes and CD-ROMs to libraries, schools, and retailers.

Distributors

Book distributors warehouse books and take orders from bookstores, retailers, libraries, etc. plus they have their own sales force that markets your books on a national basis. Expect to discount the retail price of your books 65%-70% for their services. Additional distributors are located in the Appendix at the back of this book.

Consortium Book Sales
1045 Westgate Drive
St. Paul, MN 55114
Phone: (615) 221-9035 Fax: (615) 221-0124
www.cbsd.com
Categories of interest include fiction, Hispanic, multi-cultural, drama, children, and feminism.

Culture Plus Book Distributors
291 Livingston Street
Brooklyn, NY 11217
Phone: (718) 222-9307 (310) 671-9630 fax: (718) 222-9311

Specializes in African American books

Lushena Book Distributors
1804 W. Irving Park Road
Chicago, IL 60613
Phone: (773) 975-9945 Fax: (773) 975-0045
Specializes in African American books.

Partners Book Distributing, Inc.
P. O. Box 580
Holt, MI 48842
Phone: (800) 336-3137 (517) 694-3205
Fax: (517) 694-0617/2208
Categories include African American, multi-cultural, cookbooks, travel, nature, general, and sports.

Magazines/Book Reviewers
(Additional magazines/book reviewers listed on our web site www.writershelpdesk.com)

African Voices
www.africanvoices.com

Black Enterprise
www.blackenterprise.com

Black Issues Book Review
www.blackissues.com

Ebony
www.ebony.com

Essence
www.essence.com

Heart & Soul
www.heartandsoul.com

Hispanic
www.hisp.com

Latina
www.latina.com

AsianWeek
www.asianweek.com

Mosaic
www.mosaicbooks.com

Quarterly Black Review
www.qbr.com

Upscale
www.upscalemagazine.com

Merchant Accounts/Business Credit Cards
(Other merchant accounts and credit card firms listed in LMP)

Small Publishers Association of North America (SPAN)
www.spannet.org

Publishers Marketing Association (PMA)
www.pma-online.org

Writer's Help Desk.com
www.writershelpdesk.com

National Chain Bookstores
(Other national chain bookstores listed on About.com)

Barnes & Noble
Small Print Department
122 Fifth Avenue
New York, NY 10011

Phone: 212-633-3454
Fax: 212-677-1634
www.bn.com

Books-A-Million
402 Industrial Lane
Birmingham, AL 35211-4465
Phone: 205-942-3737
www.booksamillion.com

Borders Group
100 Phoenix Drive
Ann Arbor, MI 48108
Phone: 734-477-4000
www.borders.com

Shrine Bookstore and Cultural Center
5309 M.L.K. Blvd.
Houston, TX 77021
Phone: 713-645-1071
www.shrinebookstore.com
Stores are located in Houston, Atlanta, and Detroit

Online Bookstores
(Additional online bookstores can be found on Internet)

African American Literature Book Club
www.aalbc.com

Ajani Bookstore
www.timbooktu.com/ajani.htm

Amazon.com
www.Amazon.com

Asian American Writers' Workshop
www.aaww.org

Barnes & Noble.com
www.bn.com

Cush City
www.cushcity.com

LosBestsellers.com
www.LosBestsellers.com

Mosaic Books
www.mosaicbooks.com

MyBodegacom
www.mybodega.com

Spanish Booksellers, Inc.
www.spanishbooksellers.com

WWW Virtual Library – American Indians
www.hanksville.org

Organizations/Associations
(Other literary organizations/associations listed in *Literary Market Place*)

African American Literature Book Club
Their web site offers book excerpts, poetry readings, popular and interesting new books, and links to other literary sites.
www.aalca.com

African American Mystery Page
This web site provides works on mystery, crime, and suspense fiction by African American authors and links of interest to writers.
www.aamystery.com

Asian American Writers' Workshop
The Workshop is dedicated to creating, publishing, and distributing Asian American literature. It provides several literary services that target Asian Americans.
www.aaww.org

American Black Book Writers Association
The organization states their goal for the past 20 years has been to assist black book writers and foster black books.
www.iwaysol.com/xblackbookworld.

Black Writers Alliance
This site provides a wealth of information for aspiring writers who want to develop their craft and get their work picked up by a publisher. It includes links to other valuable sites of interest to writers.
www.blackwriters.org

Black Women in Publishing
BWIP is a trade association founded to increase the presence and support the efforts of African Heritage women and men in the publishing industry.
www.bwip.org

The Go On Girl! Book Club
Monique Greenwood, Lynda Johnson, and Tracy Mitchell-Brown formed this club in 1991. Today, it is the nation's largest reading group for African American women.
www.goongirl.org

Poets & Writers (P&W)
P&W is a nonprofit organization that assists authors in their search for career-related information, outlets for their work, opportunities for professional advancement, and networking with other writers.
www.pw.org

Romance Writers of America
Today, it is the largest organization of its kind in the world, with over 8,200 members and growing.
www.rwanational.com

International Women's Writing Guild
The International Women's Writing Guild, founded in 1976, is a network for the personal and professional empowerment of women through writing.
www.iwwg.com

Women's National Book Association, Inc. (WNBA)
WNBA is a national organization of women and men who work with and value books. WNBA exists to promote reading and to support the role of women in the community of the book.
www.wnba-books.org

Writer's Help Desk.com
This site provides a wealth of information for self-published authors or literary entrepreneurs. It includes links to other valuable sites and addresses the special needs of women, African Americans, Asian Americans, Latinos, Native Americans and other minorities.
www.writershelpdesk.com

Poetry Web sites
(Additional poetry web sites listed on www.writershelpdesk.com)
Black Poets Online
Provides poetry, writing, and related links.
www.vibrantnet.com/poetry/frame.html

Nubianpoets.com
Features contests, famous poets, chat room, and resources.
www.nubianpoets.com

Poetry.com
Features instant posting of work, contests, and resources.
www.poetry.com

Timbooktu
Offers many unpublished and novice writers the opportunity to get
their work and literary resources.
www.timbooktu.com

Research

Demographics
(Additional demographics information listed in *Literary Market
Place*)

American Demographics Magazine
Gives information on ethnic consumers, including spending habits,
spending power, population, city migration, etc.
www.americandemographics.com

The Amistad Research Center
www.tulane.edu/~amistad
The Center is a manuscripts library for the study of African
American history and culture.

Book Industry Study Group (BISG)
General marketplace research firm for book buying trends.
www.bisg.org

U.S. Census Bureau
www.census.gov
Provides information on population and concentration of ethnic
groups throughout the U.S.

Schomburg Center for Research in Black Culture
A leading research center on African American and Afro-Cuban
cultures. It also feaures African American women writers of the 19th
century.
http://web.nypl.org/research/sc/sc.html

Search Engines/Directories
(Other search engines can be found on the Internet)

About®
www.about.com

Alta Vista
www.altavista.com

AOL Search
www.aol.com

BlackSeek.com
www.blackseek.com

Dogpile
www.dogpile.com

EverythingBlack.com™
www.everythingblack.com

Excite
www.excite.com

GO.com
www.go.com

HotBot
www.hotbot.com

LookSmart
www.looksmart.com

Lycos®
www.lycos.com

Northern Light
www.northernlight.com

Web Crawler
www.webcrawler.com

Yahoo!
www.yahoo.com

Web site Designers
(Additional web site designers listed on www.writershelpdesk.com)

(PageTurner.net
www.pageturner.net
They do very attractive web sites for an affordable fee.

Book Zone
www.bookzone.com

Web sites for Women – General Interest
(Other web sites for women can found on the Internet)

iVillage: information on health, parenting relationships, writing, etc.
www.ivilliage.com

Oxygen: tips on health, relationships, nutrition, work, and money.
www.oxygen.com

Oprah.com: features chat rooms, books, lifestyle resources, etc.
www.oprah.com

Women.com: offers career , small business, and lifestyle resources.
www.women.com

Top Women Sites: lists top 100 women web sites
www.100topwomensites.com

Web sites for Writers – General Interest
(Additional writers general interest web sites can be found on the Internet)

Black Voices: chats, books, black news, entertainment, etc.
www.blackvoices.com

BET.com: black entertainment, news, articles, music, etc.
www.bet.com

iVillage.com: writing resources, contests, books, chats, articles, etc.
www.ivillage.com

Netnoir: networking, reviews, gospel music
www.netnoir.com

Prolific Writers Network: book reviews, interviews, writing resources, links, etc.
www.prolificwriters.org

Tom Joyner.com: interviews, black news, music, college scholarships, etc.
www.tomjoyner.com

Wave: created for teenagers and includes poetry, music, books, book reviews, contests, etc.
www.wavemag.com

"Each of us is created to do something with our lives."

—Dennis Kimbro

Chapter 10

New Tools for the Millennium

"Books are going electronic. Some bound books will soon be as dead as the trees they are printed on.
Dan Poynter

E-Books

Electronic books or e-books are coming on strong in the 21st century. Electronic publishing is a method of producing books in various formats. They can be transferred to CD-ROMs or diskettes and read from hand-held devices. They can also be converted from text to HTML or PDF formats for sale on the Internet. The economics are different because the production and distribution costs are substantially lower. For example, there are no freight charges and no traditional book to damage or to be returned by a bookstore. Therefore, the eight times formula mentioned in Chapter 3 would probably not apply. A lower multiple would be reasonable depending on discounts given by the author or self-publisher.

Some publishers have stated e-books will eventually replace print books. Only time will truly tell whether this will hold true. Personally, we don't think they will cause the demise of print books. However, we believe e-books will be an exciting new media for the publishing industry. Imagine reading a book complemented with sound, music, animation, and colorful graphics in 3-D. Hand-held reading devices can store multiple books, thereby eliminating the inconvenience of carrying bulky and heavy books around.

What are your rights?

Electronic rights have been the subjects of much discussion. Some publishers have taken positions that their purchase of print rights also included electronic rights. For example, an author could write an article for a magazine and later find it being sold on the Internet, in CD-ROMs, or in e-books. In a recent landmark decision, the Second Circuit Court of Appeals has ruled in favor of authors.

Publishers have revised their contracts now so be sure you know what you are selling. A good copyright attorney can remove any doubt about your rights and which of your rights the contract is buying. You can also check out www.publaw.com web site for articles on electronic rights.

Many e-book publishers' contracts are straightforward. They typically purchase electronic rights for a period of one to four years. They may want to include other rights in the contract as well, such as print or audio. Be careful with selling multiple rights, especially if there are no time limits set.

Consider these before you choose an e-book publisher

Maxine Thompson, author and owner of Black Butterfly Press, an e-book publisher, states, "Publishing e-books is like the Flying Wallendas –a family of trapeze artists who performed worldwide without a net. You will lose your net –your safety and comfort zone. Although there is less financial risk involved, as an e-book publisher, you are still venturing into unknown territory, so you are afraid. However, just look at the trends of the larger publishers and it sends a louder message than your fear. You must set the rules to the game, or someone else rules". Offering e-books for your readers will allow you to reach different segments of your target audience besides a traditional paper book.

Some of the leading e-book publishers are listed below. However, they are not all the same. Some prefer to only work with publishers while others concentrate on authors. There are also differences in the ways e-book publisher compensates authors. Therefore, a checklist should be prepared with a list of questions you should ask each publisher to help you decide which publishers you should pursue. A sample list of questions follows:

1. Do you require an exclusivity agreement for my titles?
2. In which formats will my titles be made available to the buyers, e.g. PDF, HTML, print-on-demand, etc?
3. What is the royalty rate?
4. How much will I have to invest to have my book produced?
5. Do you have an established distribution network with chain bookstores and major online booksellers?
6. Do consumers need to buy a hand-held device to read the books? If yes, how much does it cost? How many e-book readers do my target audience own?
7. How many visitors come to your web site each week?
8. What major advantage does your company have over competitors?
9. How long am I obligated under your contract agreement?
10. What references can you give me?
11. How can I view some of your titles?
12. What security features do you have programmed to prevent piracy or copying?

E-Book Sources

This industry is relatively new but is rapidly evolving. For a more current list of e-book publishers and booksellers, please visit our resource site at <u>www.writershelpdesk.com</u>

Black Butterfly Press

Maxine Thompson's publishing and literary service firm offers authors e-book publishing and a variety of literary services including editing, critiquing, and Internet book marketing. She has self-published two novels, *Ebony Tree and No Pockets in a Shroud.* www.maxinethompson.com

BookLocker

This web site converts books to PDF formats and sells titles you can download from your computer. You do not have to sign an exclusivity agreement. However, you do have to pass an editorial review, so have your work edited *before* you submit your book. www.booklocker.com

Diverse eBooks

This new web site targets minorities and women who are self-published authors or literary entrepreneurs. Up to 60% royalties are paid on sales and they do not require an exclusivity agreement. They also offer marketing assistance through seminars, marketing reports, and conferences. Because they have a review process, you should not send them unedited work. Diverse eBooks is scheduled for launch in May 2001. www.diverseebooks.com

eBook

A lightweight reader device for reading books, magazines, and newspapers. Gemstar International Group Limited acquired Softbook Press and NuvoMedia, Inc in January 2000. A new reader manufactured by RCA was developed. The reading device is equipped with an elaborate encryption system to help prevent copyright infringements and piracy. Prices start from $299.00 www.ebook-gemstar.com

Fat Brain

FatBrain is a wholly-owned subsidiary of Barnes& Noble.com. Readers buy e-books from the Fatbrain web site. For their content, or eMatter, the site appears to fancy business, scientific, and technical books, although their web site also has general interest

e-books. Fatbrain also partially owns MightyWords, a popular e-book web site that lists a broad range of genres. In late 2000, the company stopped accepting most self-published authors on their web sites. There is now a review process before a work is published on their web site. This trend will probably continue with similar web sites as more focus is placed on content quality.
www.fatbrain.com

1stBooks

The company offers books in both electronic, audio, and print-on-demand formats. A national distribution network is available through Barnes&Nobel and other bookstores and online booksellers, such as Amazon.com. The minimum fee at 1stBooks is less than $1,000 for both electronic and paperback formats. Authors and publishers can elect only one format to reduce their initial publishing costs.
www.1stbooks.com

GlassBook

This software company permits readers to view e-books in PDF format. GlassBook has developed a proprietary secured format that limits the printing of documents. This software has been used by major online bookstores.
www.glassbook.com

iUniverse.com

This company has developed partnerships or alliances with Barnes and Noble (now owns 49% of the company), Ingram's Lightning Source, Writer's Digest, Writer's Club, and Author's Guild. It is positioned to be a major player in this relatively new industry.
www.iuniverse.com

Microsoft Reader®

Microsoft released its new Microsoft Reader in 2000. It uses a reader based on "Clear Type" technology. The reader is designed to display content close to the quality of paper. It is currently offering free software to use on your computer.
www.microsoft.com/reader

netLibrary

The company offers content in multiple formats that can be downloaded to desktop computers or hand-held reading devices to consumers and libraries. They also offer print-on-demand services for publishers.

www.netlibrary.com

Peanut Press

A division of netLibrary, Peanut Press focuses on the whole potential of the Palm Pilot® device. Users download book titles from their web site and then to their hand-held devices. You are not required to sign an exclusivity agreement. Royalty rates are negotiable.

www.peanutpress.com

PublishingOnline.com

This company focuses on publishers in order to offer titles in multiple formats. Their titles may be available through e-book readers or downloaded from their web site. They may also absorb the costs to convert the book titles into various formats. Manuscripts are reviewed and accepted based on content quality.

www.publishingonline.com

Versaware™

Versaware converts digital text into interactive e-books. E-books can be viewed via the Internet, DVD-ROMs, CD-ROMs, e-book readers, and other hand-held devices.

www.versaware.com

Print-on-Demand

Print-on-demand or digital printing is another exciting emerging technology. It affords the aspiring writer many advantages:

1. Only Print As Needed - print actual orders instead of estimated demand.
2. Fast Printing - books can be printed in less than two days.

3. Flexibility - books can be produced in multiple formats.
4. High Quality - digital printers produce high quality print.

Only Print-as-Needed

One of the risks of traditional printing is having books returned by bookstores. On-demand publishing cuts this risk to a minimum because the book can be printed to order. For example, digital print can be stored at a bookstore and printed only when a customer orders one. Costs associated with storing or warehousing and shipping books are reduced when books are printed only when they are needed.

Fast Printing

Imagine calling a traditional book printer with an order to produce one book within 48 hours. After they pick themselves up off the floor from laughing, they would probably say try somewhere down the street. Print-on-demand technology makes it possible to produce and deliver a book in two days or less. In some bookstores, you can now order an unprinted book, have a cup of coffee, and return to pick up your freshly printed book in 15 minutes.

Flexibility

Digital publishing is relatively simple. It is not necessary to have any printing plates prepared like traditional printing. All you need to provide the digital publisher is a PDF or PostScript file. Files can be transmitted over the Internet or delivered by mail. In this file format a book can be produced as an e-book, CD-ROM, and in soft cover or hard cover binding. You can even customize your book to suit the needs of a particular customer. For example, if a company wants a limited edition of your book printed just for them, a few minor changes in the file can produce a book with the company's name on the cover. This feature can be useful when you are trying to make premium or promotional book sales to a company. You can also have special large print editions prepared for the elderly or other niche markets.

High Quality

Digital technology produces high quality printing. The print is more consistent because density is electronically maintained. This confidence in quality is evident by the trend with major book chains buying ownership interests in on-demand book printing companies.

In a Nut Shell

In the past, a major obstacle for many writers was having enough funds to pay for printing their books in perfect-bound form. Chain bookstores and book wholesalers usually require this type of book binding, because the title is printed on a spine that can be read from a bookshelf. Print-on-demand technology has brought the cost to produce a book down substantially. Such innovations make it possible to deliver high quality books faster, in bare minimum quantities, and in soft or hardcover binding. Therefore, instead of spending $2,500 to $5,000 for your first run of books, it is possible to spend less than $500 to produce your first book. Although your price per book will be higher, you can produce fewer books to bring down your costs. As the demand for your book increases, you can then produce larger quantities using more traditional book printers at a lower cost per book.

If you are willing to sell the rights to your book to some of the digital publishing companies, you can reduce your costs to as little as $100.00. For example, iUniverse can produce an out-of-print book for approximately $100.00. Because of its partnership with Barnes and Noble, the opportunity exists to have your book available in all of the chain's stores.

On-Demand Book Printers and Services

This industry is rapidly growing. There are both new companies and established companies entering this market constantly. For a more current list of print-on-demand companies, please visit our resource site at www.writerhelpdesk.com.

iUniverse.com
620 North 48th Street, Suite 201
Lincoln, NE 68504
phone: (800) 376-1736
www.iuniverse.com
Barnes & Noble owns 49% of the company. You will probably be required to sign an exclusivity agreement, but it can be cancelled with certain provisions.

Lightning Source
1136 Heil Quaker Boulevard
LaVergne, TN 37086
phone: (615) 213-5466
fax: (615) 213-5114
www.lightningsource.com
This is a subsidiary of Ingram Industries, Inc.

Central Plains Book Manufacturing
22234 C Street, Strother Field
Winfield, KS 67156
Toll Free (877) 278-2726
Texas Sales Gary Espy (888) 411-3290
www.centralplainsbook.com

Replica Books
12000 US Highway 22 East
Bridgewater, NJ 08007
Phone: 908-429-4012
www.btol.com

Sprout, Inc.
430 Tenth Street NW, Suite S-007
Atlanta, GA 30318
phone: (404) 404-892-9600
fax: (404) 404-881-1383
www.sproutinfo.com
Borders Group has a minority interest in this company.

Trafford Publishing
2333 Government Street, Suite 6E
Victoria B.C. V8T 4P4 (Canada)
phone: (888) 232-4444
www.trafford.com

Xlibris
436 Walnut
Philadelphia, PA 19106
phone: (800) 888-795-5474 (215) 923-4686
Xlibris is a strategic partner of Random House Ventures.
www.xlibris.com

CD-ROM

CDs are becoming as popular as cassette tapes. In our fast paced and mobile society, car manufacturers equip most of their cars with CD players. Consumers can now listen to books on CDs while commuting. CDs are another alternative for individuals who do not have access to the Internet. Some e-book publishers can also produce your book in CD-ROM format. You can also burn (write or copy) them yourself if you have the proper software. Many newer desktop computers can save your file on CD's. Print software is available that will produce an attractive label for the CD. If demand for your CD-ROM is favorable, you can engage a duplicating company to print larger quantities for you to sell.

CDs can also be produced in audio instead of print or text. However, if you can combine print, audio, and video on a single CD instead of producing three separate products, substantial savings can be realized. *Words on Tape* by Judy Byers explains how to produce spoken word audio on cassettes and CDs in detail.

As the computer becomes more available in households, downloadable audio files played on MP3 and Real Audio will become another way for authors to sell their titles or information. Some individuals believe such audio files will eventually replace

CD and spoken word audios. As DVD or digital video disk players become more available in households, you can also expect DVDs to replace VHS videos.

E-Zines

E-zines are electronic publications or newsletters that are delivered by e-mail or through an online source. These publications can be free or available by paid subscriptions. The price range can vary greatly. We have seen paid subscription e-zines for as little as $3.00 and as much as $200.00. If you look hard enough, you can probably find some for much more than $200.00. The interesting thing about e-zines is that the cost to publish one is the same regardless of the price of the subscription.

What You Need to Publish E-Zines

The following equipment and services will help you produce an e-zine:

✓ Content for E-zine (information you are selling or sending)
✓ Computer
✓ E-mail Software (to maintain database of subscribers)
✓ E-mail Account
✓ Internet Service Provider (ISP)
✓ E-commerce Web site (to accept orders online)
✓ Merchant Account (to accept credit cards)
✓ Fax Machine, Software or Service (to accept orders off line)
✓ Telephone (toll free number is preferred for phone orders)

There are plenty of e-zines on the Internet. Subscribe to some of the free ones to get a feel for how they work. Decide on what subject matter you want to offer and who you want to receive the information. Offering a free newsletter in a web site is a popular way to communicate with your audience. Visit our web site at www.writershelpdesk.com for sources for web site design, merchant accounts, web hosting service providers and other resources to help you with your project.

Internet

The Internet is making life for self-published and traditionally published authors a lot easier. This advantage will only improve in the 21st century. Authors can market their books online through booksellers such as Amazon.com or Barnes & Noble.com (bn.com). E-books will also become more popular on these and other web sites. Many authors are also setting up their own personal sites. For example, we have one at www.sarafreemansmith.com that announces speaking engagements, book events, and sells our books and consulting services.

The Internet is also an excellent resource for research. Take advantage of resources such as newsgroups and trade associations that provide valuable information for your book project. The Internet is mentioned throughout this book, so you might want to review some of the other chapters. If you have not purchased a computer or other access device, you need to do so and learn how to take advantage of all that the Internet has to offer.

Newsgroups

Newsgroups are Internet discussion groups or forums, consisting of individuals with a common subject interest. They can be a no or low cost way to begin to position yourself as an expert in your industry. They are *not* intended for you to use as an advertising outlet. If you try to advertise in chat rooms or on message boards, prepare to get flamed. Flamed is a term used to describe nasty emails you get from newsgroups when you break the rules. Imagine getting so many e-mails that they shut down your whole e-mail system. It could happen if you openly violate their rules.

A good source to find newsgroups is www.deja.com. You can also find newsgroup links on the home pages of many browsers and search engines. If your book is on fishing, look for a fishing newsgroup. If your book is a science fiction novel, look for a science fiction group. Once you join a newsgroup, observe the discussions before you join the talks. This will help you become familiar with how they operate, thus reducing the risk of getting flamed or kicked out of the group. When you are comfortable with the group, then you can join in on the discussions. Some groups will allow you to mention your name, company, e-mail, and web site address when you make a worthwhile contribution to a discussion. However, you should be certain this is acceptable to the group first. When you are able to give your URL or web site address, some group members may visit your site and purchase your books or other products.

Op-In E-mail Lists

Mailing lists are a great way to build a database of potential buyers. E-mail lists are a no cost or low cost way to get information to your buying audience. However, e-mail should be sent to individuals who have given you permission to e-mail them. This is normally done when a person signs up or subscribes to your mailing list. For example, if you sign up on a web site for a free newsletter, you have opted to be placed in the mailing list database.

If you start sending e-mails to individuals who have not given you permission to send them e-mails, this is known as spamming. Your Internet Service Provider (ISP) may terminate your service if you get spamming complaints from their customers or other parties.

Chapter 11

Dynamic Literary Organizations

As literary entrepreneurs or self-published authors, we have many allies willing to help us write, publish, support, promote, and sell our books. These organizations have a wealth of resources and services that are vital for your success. This section features some of these dynamic organizations. Others are listed in the Appendix and chapters of this book. Occasionally we will feature some of these groups in the Writer's Help Desk.com web site at www.writershelpdesk.com. We urge you to support these groups and their causes. Without them your journey to a successful book will certainly be much more difficult.

The African American Book Club Summit
www.summitatsea.com

The African American Book Club Summit is an annual national effort to form an alliance among African American Book Clubs, Authors, and Independent Booksellers.

In October 2000, the group organized a cruise from Galveston, Texas to Cancun and Cozumel Mexico. This event brought together African American authors and avid readers from across the country for a 5-day conference to promote reading for pleasure and writing as a career goal. Numerous workshops to inform and encourage up-and-coming writers as well as forums for cruise participants to meet their favorite authors were conducted. We conducted a workshop on self-publishing.

Both published authors and literary entrepreneurs participated in this highly attended event through workshops and book signings. This was a great opportunity for authors to sell their books and network with people vital to their success.

The event for 2001 will be a 7-day cruise from New Orleans, Louisiana to Cozumel, Grand Cayman , and Montego Bay. We hope to see you there.

African American Women on Tour (AAWOT)
www.aawot.com

This 10 year old organization is one of the premier support networks for African American women . It provides a forum for uplifting, empowering, and enhancing the quality of life for black women.

By conducting tobacco-free and alcohol-free conferences in six major U.S. cities, AAWOT presents over 150 workshops on business and career development, financial management, family relations, health, and Rites of Passage programs. Their conferences featuring, internationally recognized speakers, celebrities, authors, and poets, attract over 5,000 women from across the country.

AAWOT present a unique opportunity for women writers and poets to promote their literary works. Their workshops and author signings present an excellent venue for authors and poets to network and get acquainted with their reading audience. For more information on their conferences, visit their web site or contact them at:

African American Women on Tour
6297 Del Cerro Blvd.
San Diego, CA 92120
Phone: (800) 560-AAWT (2298)
www.aawot.com

Black Writers Alliance (formerly African American Online Writers Guild)
www.blackwriters.org

Founded by Tia Shabazz, The Black Writers Alliance (BWA) is dedicated to providing information, news, resources and support to Black writers while promoting the Internet as a tool for research and fellowship among the cultural writing community.

COMMUNITY: Blackwriters.org offers numerous opportunities for writers to connect with others who share their passion for the written word through discussion lists, message boards, chats, pen pal listings, writing and critique groups, events, the web ring and the efforts of the BWA Community Representatives and volunteers. Through Blackwriters.org, writers of African descent in the U.S., the Caribbean and around the world are able to meet, interact with, encourage, inspire, and learn from one another.

CONTENT: Within this site are published listings of Black agents, publicists, editors, publishing companies, publishing consultants, newspapers, and magazines, plus a newsletter, which contains BWA news, conference reports, site updates, online and literary events, authors' news, tips, tidbits, and more. But the most valuable, timely, and useful content is offered directly to members' e-mail inboxes via the Black Writers Alliance's Blackwriters-L e-mail list.

CULTURE: The BWA celebrates the strength of our heritage, the beauty and richness of our culture and the spirit of our ancestors by supporting the efforts, growth, and achievements of fellow Black literary artists and striving to expand appreciation of the Black literary tradition.

"Our members make up the largest interactive community of Black writers on the Internet, "says Tia Shabazz, BWA Executive Director. Although founded for and dedicated to the needs of Black writers, the Black Writers Alliance does not discriminate on the basis of race, color or creed.

CONFERENCE: The Black Writers Reunion & Conference is an annual gathering of creative minds, bodies and spirits in celebration of written expression, and commitment to the nurturing of Black writers in furtherance of Black literature. This weekend event offers a 50-Author Expo, the Authors' Reception, the Poets' Reception, over 25 workshops, panel discussions, the inspirational Sunday brunch, and networking with writers, agents, editors, and publishers from all over the country. The Gold Pen Awards Banquet will honor the achievements of eight African-American authors of fiction, nonfiction, and poetry and the Vanguard Award to an exemplary African American professional who has made outstanding contributions to Black literature. The banquet will also feature entertaining skits from plays to scenes from featured authors' books, to comedy, music, and poetry. By the way, the 2001 event will be held August 3-5 in Dallas, Texas. We hope to see you there. Check out their web site for more details.

Asian American Writers' Workshop
www.aaww.org

The Asian American Writers' Workshop, Inc is a nonprofit organization that is headquartered in New York City. The Workshop is dedicated to creating, publishing, and distributing Asian American literature. It provides several literary services that target Asian Americans. It publishes *The Asian Pacific American Journal* and *Ten,* a literary magazine. The organization also offers the following:
- Literary readings
- Fellowships to aspiring Asian American writers
- Creative writing workshops facilitated by award-winning artists
- Performances
- The Annual Asian American Literary Awards
  CreateNow —a youth program

The Workshop also operates The Asian American Bookseller. According to the Workshop, this bookstore is the most comprehensive collection of Asian American books and magazines in the country.

Asian American Writers' Workshop
16 West 32nd Street, Suite 10A
New York, NY 10001
Phone: (212) 494-0061 Fax: (212) 494-0062
E-mail: desk@aaww.org

Black Women In Publishing, Inc. (BWIP)
www.bwip.org

Black Women in Publishing is a trade association founded to increase the presence and support the efforts of African Heritage women and men in the publishing industry. BWIP was established in 1979 by a group of African American women who recognized the benefit of networking for successful careers and is open to anyone interested in the world of books, magazines, newspapers, newsletters, and interactive media.

They state their goals are realized through meetings and publications which:

- Facilitate learning and networking forums
- Provide career growth and entrepreneurial opportunities
- Recognize initiative and achievement

BWIP members can be found in human resources, editorial and management, finance and production, art and design, marketing and sales, and wholesale and retail. They are writers, publishers, freelancers, agents, attorneys, CEOs, VPs, and business owners.

Detroit Writer's Guild (Formerly the Detroit Black Writer's Guild)
www.blackarts-literature.org

The Detroit Writer's Guild was founded in 1982 by Peggy A. Moore. It is one of the oldest organizations of its type in the country. In the beginning, it was a backyard literary club. However, today it is a national organization with over 450 members in 24 states. The organization lists its mission as follows:

- Nurture the creative drive of African-Americans and other ethnic groups in the cultural arts.
- Serve as a forum for networking
- Provide a database for writers and artists resources and grants.
- Serve as a marketing tool for writers and authors.
- Serve as a communications hub for related arts organizations.
- Serve as a bulletin board for freelance job opportunities.
- Provide a database of related activities around the country such as conference, contests, special events, etc.
- Design and host web pages for individuals and cultural arts organizations.

The Good Book Club
www.goodbookclub.com

According to the club's President, Pam Walker-Williams, The Good Book Club was founded in 1998 by a group of friends in the Houston-Clear Lake, Texas area. The first meeting was held in March 1998, the group discussed, "If This World Were Mine" by E. Lynn Harris.

In August 1998, the club launched its web site and opened membership up to the global World Wide Web Community. Currently, they have over 300 cyber members throughout the United States, Canada, and Germany.

The Go On Girl! Book Club
www.goongirl.org

Monique Greenwood, Lynda Johnson, and Tracy Mitchell-Brown formed this club in 1991. Today, it is the nation's largest reading group for African American women, with 32 chapters and growing.

The Club lists its goals on it web site as follows:
- To expand the members' personal literary experience by:

    Reading quality works written by authors of African descent
    Reading a selection of titles that vary in genre from new and classic fiction to science-fiction/fantasy and mystery to social commentary and history to autobiographies/biographies

- To encourage responsible writing & publishing of literature written by people of African descent by:

    Sending book reviews and letters of encouragement to authors and publishers
    Presenting recognition awards
    Purchasing books written and edited by people of African descent
    Supporting literary affairs
    Making group investments towards worthy literary affairs

- To provide an open forum for the exchange of ideas & opinions by:
    Having monthly book discussions
    Networking with other book clubs and literary societies at least once a year

- To expose the African-American community at large to literature written by people of African descent by:

Sponsoring Junior Go On Girl! Book Clubs for high school girls. Hosting/sponsoring literary events on our own or jointly with other organizations or institutions.

National Headquarters
P.O. Box 3368
New York, NY 10185
www.goongirl.org

Milligan Books
www.milliganbooks.com

Since its founding in 1990, Milligan Books has skyrocketed to become the fastest growing Black female-owned publishing company in America. The company has published more than 50 Black authors. Several of their works have made various bestseller lists.

"There are many talented and dedicated Black writers," says Dr. Rosie Milligan, founder and owner of Milligan Books, "who have written well-crafted works that deserve publication". Dr. Milligan emphasizes that she is not in competition with the mainstream publishers, many of whom she feels publish excellent works. Her mission simply is to offer authors another opportunity to reach an audience with their work. She is a featured columnist in *Black Issues Magazine*.

Contact: Dr. Rosie Milligan   DrRosie@aol.com
323-750-3592 (Phone)   www.milliganbooks.com

Poets & Writers (P&W)
www.pw.org

Poets & Writers is a nonprofit organization that assists authors in their search for career-related information, outlets for their work, opportunities for professional advancement, and networking with other writers.

For over 30 years, P&W has provided support and exposure to writers throughout the various stages of their development. They reported disbursing $175,000 in 2000 to over 800 writers, reaching 130,000 people. P&W are not a membership organization, so anyone may use their services.

For more information on this progressive organization, you may contact them at:

Poets & Writers
72 Spring Street
New York, NY 10012;
Phone:(212) 226-3586 Fax: (212) 226-3963.
www.pw.org

Publishers Marketing Association (PMA)
www.pma-online.org

Publishers Marketing Association (PMA) is the country's largest trade association of independent publishers. Founded in 1983, it serves book, audio, and video publishers located in the United States and around the world.

Its mission is to advance independent publishing through professional development, creative marketing, and global affiliation. To this end, PMA provides numerous benefits, including: wholesaler acceptance assistance, cooperative marketing programs, discounts on publishers liability insurance, vendor discount benefits, seminars, merchant accounts, a monthly newsletter, health insurance programs, and advocacy within the publishing industry.

Publishers Marketing Association
627 Aviation Way
Manhattan Beach, CA 90266
phone: 310-372-2732 · fax: 310-374-3342
e-mail: info@pma-online.org

Romance Writers Association
www.rwanational.com

Romance Writers of America is a nonprofit genre writers' association that was founded in Houston, Texas in 1980. After attending writing conferences that failed to address the needs of romance writers, the 37 founding members decide to take action. They organized writing conferences designed especially for romance writers, created a national networking and support group of romance writers. They provided romance writers a voice to deal with the daunting New York publishers. Today, it is the largest organization of its kind in the world, with over 8,200 members and growing.

Each summer the Romance Writers of America hosts a national conference in a U.S. city. The organization conducts more than 100 workshops with various topics ranging from beginning writing skills to writing as a business. During this event, one-on-one interviews are scheduled with editors and literary agents who are seeking new talent. In 2001, the National Conference will be held in New Orleans, Louisiana.

Organization members include actors, artists, attorneys, businesswomen, doctors, engineers, mathematicians, military officers, musicians, scientists, stay-at-home mothers, teachers, and many other professions. In 1999, RWA had more than 120 worldwide chapters with at least one chapter in almost every state in the United States. There are three chapters in Houston, Texas where the organization was first formed. . If you are seriously pursuing a career in romance fiction, be sure to contact this literary group.

3707 FM 1960 West, Suite 555
Houston, TX 77068
Phone: (281) 440-6885 Fax: (281) 440-7510
www.rwanational.com

Conclusion

"If you don't have the time to read, you don't have the time or the tools to write."
Stephen King

Congratulations, you made it through the book! Now, don't stop here. Your journey has just begun. You should begin to choose some of the tools provided in this book. Also, buy some of the recommended books or go to the library and check out as many reference books on self-publishing as possible. This book will help you publish your book and target your message to the audience that you want to reach. Remember, you can have a great book, but no one will know that until they read it. Make sure you develop a marketing plan that targets the people who want to buy it.

Believe in yourself and your book. Always maintain the passion for your book. See yourself achieving your goal daily. You will face obstacles on your journey, but you now have ways to detour and go around them. You must continue to take action and turn your dreams into reality.

"I have learned that success is to be measured not so much by the position that one has reached in life as by the obstacles which one has overcome while trying to succeed."

Booker T. Washington

Afterword

By Sara Freeman Smith,
Co-Author & Publisher, *How To Self-Publish & Market Your Own Book*
Author of *Turning Stones Into Gems*

How to Self-Publish & Market Your Own Book – Second Edition contains proven methods to successfully publish what you've written. It is a self-help and publishing tool. Countless hours on the computer, telephone calls, attending conferences, meetings with publishing professionals, and extensive research brought our book to fruition. The success of our first book and gratitude journal, *Turning Stones Into Gems,* would not have been possible without Mack's business acumen and hard work. All that hard work finally paid off and led us to ultimately write this book.

By publishing our books, we learned a lot and now share this knowledge with you and other aspiring writers. We learned the road to success is a journey, not a destination, and it's an uphill road at that! You will always face obstacles on your journey to success, but begin to look for a way **around, over, under,** or **through them!** Do not let them stop you from achieving your dream. After all, a dream is merely a goal that's not written down or yet accomplished. Remember; watch out for big obstacles in your path, they usually turn out to be big opportunities for success.

We want to help you accomplish your dream. Our desire is to help enough people achieve their goals in life, so we, in turn, achieve success, too. *How to Self-Publish & Market Your Own Book* will give you a map and explain how to use the tools. Now, you can begin your successful journey to publishing your book. Always remember that the God of the *vision* will be the God of *provision*! God only makes originals, never a copy!

You are a Gem!
May God bless you in all your endeavors.

Appendix

Resource Guide

Traditional Book Schedule

Sample Forms

Resource Guide

Bar Codes
(Additional bar codes firms are listed in the *Literary Market Place*)

Fotel, Inc.
41 West Home Avenue
Villa Park, IL 60181
Phone: (800) 834-4920
Fax: (630) 834-5250
www.fotel.com

Bar Code Graphics, Inc.
Phone: (800) 662-0701
Fax: (312) 664-4939
www.barcode-graphics.com

General Graphics
Box 3192
Arnold, PA 15068-0992
Phone: (800) 887-5894
Phone: (724) 337-1470
Fax: (724) 337-6589
E-Mail: ggbarcode@aol.com

Book Clubs
(Additional book clubs can be found in the *Literary Market Place*)

The Book-of-the-Month Clubs
(Children's & Quality Paperback Clubs)
Phone (212) 522-4200
www.bomc.com

The Literary Guild & Doubleday Direct Inc.
Phone (212) 782-7200
www.literaryguild.com

Oprah's Book Club
www.oprah.oxygen.com/obc/obc_landing.html

Writer's Digest Book Club
Phone (800) 289-0963
www.writersdigest.com

Book Consultants
(Additional book consultants found in the *Literary Market Place*)

Open Horizons
John Kremer (515) 472-6130
www.bookmarket.com

Para Publishing
Dan Poynter (805) 968-7277
www.parapublishing.com

U R Gems Group
Mack E. Smith & Sara Freeman Smith (281) 596-8330
www.urgems.com

Book Cover Designers
(Other book cover designers listed on www.writershelpdesk.com)

Gladys Ramirez, (She designed our book covers)
Phone: (713) 298-2206
E-mail: gladys.ramirez@earthlink.net

Volume Media, Inc., Marc Newsome
Phone: (713) 781-4650
www.volumemediainc.com

Yorké Design, Mary Valle-Cooper
Phone: (281) 485-7138
E-mail: yorkedesign@ev1.net.

Juanita Cole Howard
www.PageTurner.net/Juanita
E-mail: jhowardart@aol.com

Book Covers
Phone (800) 449-4095
www.bookcovers.com

Book Distribution Resources

Book wholesalers only

Baker & Taylor Books
Phone: (908) 218-0400
www.btol.com

One of the nation's largest book wholesalers. Distributes books nationally and has special markets such as the Christian market, gift markets, and libraries.

Ingram Book Company
Phone: (615) 793-5000
www.ingrambookgroup.com
Ingram is one of the nation's largest book wholesalers. They are a premier supplier to national book chains, libraries, and schools.

Exclusive Distributors and Wholesalers
(Some firms handle both relationships; contact each regarding specific criteria requirements). Be sure to check out each company for credit history, payment terms, discounts, etc. A complete listing of exclusive distributors can be located in the *Literary Market Place.*

Associated Publisher's Group
Phone: (800) 327-5113
www.apgbooks.com
Distributes books nationally and has special markets such as the Christian and gift markets.

Bookazine
Phone (800) 221-8112
www.bookazine.com
National wholesalers for small presses.

BookWorld Services, Inc.
Phone: (813) 758-8094
www.bookworld.com
Wholesalers/distributor for small presses with more than two titles.

Hervey's Booklink
Phone (214) 221-2711 Fax: (214) 221-2715
www.herveys.com
Wholesalers/distributors for small publishers and specialty
marketing for cookbooks.

Independent Publishers Group (IPG)
Phone: (312) 337-0747 Fax: (312) 337-5985
www.ipgbook.com
They are the oldest independent distributor. PMA has a special
program with them for small presses.

Partners Book Distributing, Inc.
Phone (800) 336-3137
National distributors for small presses.

Partners/West Book Distributing Inc.
Phone (800) 563-2385
Wholesaler for large and small presses.

Publishers Group West
Phone: (510) 658-3453
www.pgw.com
The largest marketing and distribution company for independent
publishers.

Quality Books, Inc.
Phone (800) 323-4241 Fax (815) 732-4499
www.quality-books.com
National distributors to libraries for small presses.

Spring Arbor Distributors
Phone (800) 395-4340
www.springarbor.com
National Christian distributor owned by Ingram

Unique Books
Phone: (800) 533-5446
E-mail: uniquebks@aol.com
National distributors to libraries for small presses.

Book Editors
(Other book editors listed on www.writershelpdesk.com)

Chandra Sparks Taylor
Phone: (718) 341-3688
E-mail: cstedit1@aol.com or curtshamjam@aol.com

Judy King
Phone: (713) 721-3003;
E-mail: judyking@pdq.net.)

Melanie Malinowsky, PhD
Email:MMalinowsk@aol.com.

Sonya Vann (she edited our second edition)
E-mail:sonyavann@yahoo.com

Book Fulfillment Services
(Additional fulfillment firms are listed in the *Literary Market Place*)

Book Clearing House
46 Purdy Street

Harrison, NY 10528
Phone: (914) 835-0015 Fax: (914) 835-0398
www.book-clearing-house.com

BookMasters, Inc.
P.O. Box 2139
Mansfield, OH 44905
Phone: (800) 537-6727 Fax: (419) 589-4040
www.bookmasters.com

PSI Fulfillment, Inc.
8803 Tara Lane
Austin, TX 78737
Phone: (800) 460-0500 Fax: (512) 288-5055
www.psifulfillment.com

Book Printers

Many book printers have book warehousing, order fulfillment, cover design services, etc. Be sure to ask for information about all of their publishing services. Additional printers are listed in *Literary Market Place.*

Alpha Publishing Group
12651 Briar Forest
Houston, Texas 77077 Phone: (281) 493-2993
www.alphapublishing.com
A print broker

Bookcrafters
P.O. Box 370
Chelsea, MI 48118-0370
Phone: (313) 475-9145 Fax: (313) 475-7337
www.bookcrafters.com

BookMasters
P.O. Box 2139

Mansfield, OH 44905
Phone: (800) 537-6727 Fax: (419) 589-4040
www.bookmasters.com

Central Plains Book Manufacturing
2498 Lakefront Shores
Athens, TX 75751
Phone: (888) 411-3290 Fax: (903) 677-7310
Gary Espy Account Representative
Competitive pricing and they printed this edition.
www.centralplainsbook.com

McNaughton & Gunn, Inc
960 Woodland Drive Saline, MI 42176
Phone: (734) 429-5411 Fax: (800) 677-2665
http://www.bookprinters.com

Morris Publishing
3212 E. Hwy 30
Kearney, NE 68847
Phone: (800) 650-7888 Fax: (308) 237-0263
www.morrispublishing.com
Custom book printing and can do small quantities

Patterson Printing
1550 Territorial Road
Benton Harbor, MI 49022-1937
Phone: (800) 848-8826 Fax: (616) 925-6057
www.patterson-printing.com

R J Communications LLC
Phone: (800) 621-2556 East Coast
Phone: (800) 754-7089 West Coast
www.booksjustbooks.com
Offer instant print estimates online.

Whitehall Printing Company
4244 Corporate Square

Naples, FL 34104-4753
Phone: (800) 321-9290 Fax: (941) 643-6439
www.whitehallprinting.com
Very competitive short-run prices

Book Printers- Print-on-Demand

(Additional print-on-demand printers listed on
www.writershelpdesk.com)

iUniverse.com
620 North 48th Street, Suite 201
Lincoln, NE 68504
Phone: (800) 376-1736
www.iuniverse.com
Barnes & Noble owns 49% of the company. You will probably be
required to sign an exclusivity agreement, but it can be cancelled
with certain provisions.

Lightning Source
1136 Heil Quaker Boulevard
LaVergne, TN 37086
Phone: (615) 213-5466
Fax: (615) 213-5114
www.lightningprint.com
This is a subsidiary of Ingram Industries, Inc.

Replica Books
12000 US Highway 22 East
Bridgewater, NJ 08007
Phone: 908-429-4012
www.btol.com

Sprout, Inc.
430 Tenth Street NW, Suite S-007
Atlanta, GA 30318
Phone: (404) 404-892-9600
www.sproutinfo.com
Borders Group has a minority interest in Sprout, Inc.

Trafford Publishing
2333 Government Street, Suite 6E
Victoria B.C. V8T 4P4 (Canada)
Phone: (888) 232-4444
www.trafford.com

Xlibris
436 Walnut
Philadelphia, PA 19106
Phone: (800) 888-795-5474 (215) 923-4686
Xlibris is a strategic partner of Random House Ventures.
www.xlibris.com

Book Packagers

Rita Mills – Morris-Mills Publishing
www.mills-morrispublishing.com
A book packager working specifically with nonprofits to produce
books for fundraising and outreach. A consultant for Asian book
printers. E-mail: rmills@ghgcorp.com

Book Reviewers

Book reviewers typically require pre-publication copies or galleys
three to five months in advance:

Publishers Weekly
Phone: (212) 463-6631
www.publishersweekly.com

Library Journal
Phone: (212) 463-6819
www.libraryjournal.com

The Los Angeles Times Magazine
Phone: (213) 237-7811
www.latimes.com

The New York Times Book Review
Phone: (212) 556-1234
www.nytimes.com

Romantic Times
Phone (718) 237-1097
www.romantictimes.com

USA Today
Phone (703) 276-3400
www.usatoday.com

Additional book review resources can be found in the *Literary Market Place* and look in your favorite magazines.

Business Research Data

U.S. General Book Store (Government Printing Office)
Information on trademarks, copyrights, demographics, and other resources. Web site has online ordering and bookstore locations.
http://bookstore.gpo.gov

Book Industry Study Group (BISG)
General marketplace research firm for book buying trends.
www.bisg.org

Directories
(Additional directories found in the library)

Bacon's Newspaper/Magazine Directory
Lists trade and consumer magazines, daily & weekly newspapers and radio & TV stations.
This directory can be located in most libraries.

Radio-TV Interview Report
Bradley Communication Corp.

135 E. Plumstead Ave,
Lansdowne, PA 19050
Phone: (610) 259-1070
This newsletter is sent to thousands of TV and radio producers.

Gale Directory of Publication & Broadcast Media
This directory lists newspapers, magazines, and journals in USA &
Canada along with feature editors at daily newspapers. It also lists
radio/TV and cable stations. This directory can be located in most
libraries.

Literary Market Place
Phone: (800) 521-8110
www.literarymarketplace.com
This reference book lists news services, feature syndicates, printers,
wholesalers, book clubs & book reviewers for newspapers and
magazines, radio/TV programs which feature books. Check with
your local library for a copy.

Standard Periodical Directory
This reference publication lists thousands of magazines, journals,
newsletters, directories, and association publications. Check with
your local library for a copy.

Writer's Market
This book is a great resource for most writers and can be found in
libraries or bookstores. It lists contact information on book
publishers, magazines, small presses, book producers, etc. It tells
you where to sell your literary works.

E-Book Publishers & Readers
(Additional e-book publishers & readers listed on
www.writershelpdesk.com)

Black Butterfly Press (Maxine Thompson's website)
www.maxinethompson.com

BookLocker
www.booklocker.com

Diverse eBooks
www.diverseebooks.com

eBook (a reader)
www.ebook-gemstar.com

Fat Brain
www.fatbrain.com

1stBooks
www.1stbooks.com

GlassBook (a reader)
www.glassbook.com

iUniverse.com
www.iuniverse.com

Microsoft Reader® (a reader)
www.microsoft.com/reader

netLibrary
www.netlibrary.com

Peanut Press
www.peanutpress.com

PublishingOnline.com
www.publishingonline.com

Versaware™
www.versaware.com

Government Agencies
(Government agencies servicing writing interests)

Register of Copyrights
Library of Congress
Washington, DC 20559-6000
Phone: (800) 688-9889
Phone: (202) 707-3000
www.loc.gov/copyright/forms

Government Information Web site
www.info.gov

Federal Trade Commission
Washington, DC 20580
Phone: (202) 326-2222
www.ftc.gov

U.S. Patent and Trademark Office
Phone: (703) 308-HELP
www.uspto.gov

SCORE
Phone: (800) 634-0245
A nonprofit organization that partners with the SBA to counsel
small businesses through retired entrepreneurs.
www.score.org

Small Business Administration (SBA)
Phone: (800) 827-5722
Call or visit web site for a branch near you.
www.sba.gov

Grants, Awards, and Contests
(Additional grants, awards and contests found on About.com)

American Library Association
www.ala.org

American Poets Fund
Academy of American Poets
www.poets.org

Associated Writing Programs
www.awpwriter.org

Carnegie Corporation of New York
www.carnegie.org

The Foundation Center
www.fdncenter.org

National Endowment for the Arts
www.arts.endow.gov

PEN American Center
www.pen.org

Poets & Writers
www.pw.org

Writer's Digest
www.writersdigest.com

Library Locations

American Library Directory
R. R. Bowker
Phone: (888) 269-5372
www.bowker.com
USA & Canadian libraries listing and can be found in the library.

Marketing/Publicity/Promotions
(Additional book marketing and book promotions sources listed on www.writershelpdesk.com)

Authorlink
www.authorlink.com

Three G Communications
Janice Gibson (713) 686-6106
www.threegcommunications.com

The Raleigh Group
Raleigh Pinskey
Phone: (561) 967-0447
www.promoteyourself.com

MarketAbility
Phone: (303) 279-4349
www.marketability.com

KSB Promotions
Phone: (616) 676-0758
E-mail: KSBPromo@aol.com

National Chain Bookstores
(Additional chain bookstores listed on About.com)

Barnes & Noble
Small Print Department
122 Fifth Avenue
New York, NY 10011
Phone: (212) 633-3454 Fax: (212) 677-1634
www.bn.com

Books-A-Million
402 Industrial Lane
Birmingham, AL 35211-4465

Phone: 205-942-3737
www.booksamillion.com

Borders Group
100 Phoenix Drive
Ann Arbor, MI 48108
Phone: 734-477-4000
www.borders.com

Chapters, Inc
90 Ronson Dr.
Toronto, ON M9W 1C1 Canada
www.chaptersinc.com

Family Christian Stores
5300 Patterson Ave., SE
Grand Rapids, MI 49530
www.familychristian.com

WaldenBooks
100 Phoenix Drive
Ann Arbor, MI 48108
www.waldenbooks.com

Newletters/E-Zines
(Additional newsletters/e-zines listed on www.writershelpdesk.com)

Book Marketing Update
www.bookmarket.com

Publishing Poynters
www.parapub.com

Writers Help Desk
www.writershelpdesk.com

Online Bookstores
(Additional online bookstores listed on About.com)

Amazon.com
www.Amazon.com

Asian American Writers' Workshop
www.aaww.org

Barnes & Noble.com
www.bn.com

Book-A-Million.com
www.bamm.com

Borders
www.borders.com

Cush City
www.cushcity.com

LosBestsellers.com
www.LosBestsellers.com

Mosaic Books
www.mosaicbooks.com

MyBodega.com
www.mybodega.com

Spanish Booksellers, Inc.
www.spanishbooksellers.com

WWW Virtual Library – American Indians
www.hanksville.org

Professional Assistance

Ivan Hoffman Trademark & Copyright Attorney
www.ivanhoffman.com

The Publishing Law Center

www.publaw.com
Publishing Law Center resource where you can find articles on legal issues that pertain to publishers, editors, and authors.

Professional Associations
(Additional professional trade associations can be found in the *Literary Market Place*)

American Booksellers Association
Phone: (800) 637-0037
www.ambook.org

American Library Association
Phone: (312) 944-6780
www.ala.org
They sponsor important conferences for the library industry and sell library mailing lists by library type.

American Society of Journalists and Authors
1501 Broadway, Suite 302
New York, NY 10036
Phone: 212-997-0947 Fax: 212-768-7414
It is the nation's leading organization of independent nonfiction. writers.

Association of Authors and Publishers
P.O. Box 35038
Houston, TX 77235-5038
www.authorsandpublishers.org

This local group is well organized and consists of published and self-published authors, small presses, editors, book packagers, indexers, translators, and other literary professionals.

Austin Writers' League
1501 W. 5th Street, Suite E-2
Austin, TX 78703
Phone: (512) 499-8914 Fax: (512) 499-0441
www.writersleague.org
The mission of the Austin Writers' League is to promote literature and celebrate the written word as art by providing educational and technical assistance to writers — from beginning to professional — and to serve as an umbrella and public clearinghouse for literary activity in Texas.

The Authors Guild
31 East 28th Street, 10th Floor
New York, NY 10016
Phone: (212) 563-5904 Fax: (212) 564-5363
www.authorsguild.org
This group is the nation's largest society of published authors.

Christian Writers Fellowship International
1624 Jefferson Davis Rd.
Clinton, SC 29325
Phone: 864-697-6035
www.cwfi-online.org

Horror Writers Association
P.O. Box 50577
Palo Alto, CA 94303
E-mail: hwa@horror.org
www.horror.org

Mystery Writers of America
17 E. 47th St., 6th Floor,
New York, NY 10017
Phone: (212) 888-8171 Fax (212) 888-8107

www.mysterywriters.net
It is considered the premier organization for mystery writers and other professionals in the mystery field.

Poets & Writers (P&W)
72 Spring Street
New York, NY 10012
Phone: (212) 226-3586; Fax (212) 226-3963.
www.pw.org
Since its founding in 1970, P&W has provided a broad range of resources to the literary community.

Publishers Marketing Association (PMA)
Phone: (310) 372-2732
www.pma-online.org
This national trade association caters to small presses and self-publishers.

Romance Writers of America
3707 FM 1960 West, Suite 555
Houston, TX 77068
Phone: (281) 440-6885 Fax: (281) 440-7510
www.rwanational.com
The organization conducts more than 100 workshops with various topics ranging from beginning writing skills to writing as a business.

Science Fiction and Fantasy Writers of America
1436 Altamont Ave., PMB 292
Schenectady, NY 12303-2977
www.sfwa.org
The organization was founded in 1965 and has over 1,200 members.

Small Publishers Association of North America (SPAN)
Phone: (719) 395-4790
www.spannet.org
This national trade association caters to small presses and self-publishers.

The Society of Children's Book Writers & Illustrators
Phone: (323) 782-1010 Fax: (323) 782-1892
www.scbwi.org
This national organization is the largest of its kind in the world.

Publishing Magazines
(Additional publishing magazines can be located in the *Literary Market Place*)

ALA Booklist
www.ala.org/booklist

Bookselling This Week
www.ambook.org

ForeWord
www.forewordmagazine.com

Library Journal
www.libraryjournal.com

Publishers Weekly
www.publishersweekly.com

Writer's Digest
www.writersdigest.com

Search Engines
(Additional search engines found on the Internet)

About®
www.about.com

Alta Vista
www.altavista.com

AOL Search
www.aol.com

BlackSeek.com
www.blackseek.com

Dogpile
www.dogpile.com

EverythingBlack.com™
www.everythingblack.com

Excite
www.excite.com

GO.com
www.go.com

HotBot
www.hotbot.com

LookSmart
www.looksmart.com

Lycos®
www.lycos.com

Northern Light
www.northernlight.com

Web Crawler
www.webcrawler.com

Yahoo!
www.yahoo.com

Web site Designers

(Additional web site designers listed on www.writershelpdesk.com)

PageTurner.net
www.pageturner.net
They do very attractive web sites for an affordable fee.

BookZone
www.bookzone.com

Writing Craft Resources
(Additional writing craft resources on www.writershelpdesk.com)

Writer's Digest.com
www.writersdigest.com

Inkspot
www.inkspot.com

You Can Write
www.youcanwrite.com

Appendix

Traditional Book Schedule

Traditional Book Production Schedule

This book production schedule will help you stay focused and on track with traditional book printing. E-books and on-demand publishing will have different schedules. You may want to make your own adjustments as you gain more experience in publishing.

Timing is a critical element in avoiding unnecessary delays in producing a book. For example, you need to obtain certain information before you can finish a cover design. The cover design can take as much as three months to complete. If you wait until you are almost ready to send your book to the printer, you may find yourself three months behind schedule. Certain registrations take several weeks, if you don't apply for them ahead of time, they may further delay you.

Traditional Book Schedule Sample

First Month	Before Writing Your Manuscript
	Determine your selling price. Follow steps in Chapter 3 *Taking Care of Business* as a guide.
	Review our web site, www.writershelpdesk.com and Appendix for additional books, reports for your book project.
	Join a publishers association (See Appendix) for helpful resources and contacts.
	Select a name for your company or publishing firm.
	Secure a mailing address for your business. Rent a P. O. Box or mailbox.
	Research where you can file your assumed name certificate, fictitious business name statement, or DBA (Doing Business As). This is usually processed at a City, County/Parish Courthouse for a nominal fee.
	Design and develop your business forms: letterhead, business cards, envelopes, and fax cover sheets.
	Begin developing a marketing plan for your book. Refer to Chapter 8 for details.
	Consult your local Small Business Association, Chamber of Commerce, banker, CPA, or attorney for planning advice.
	Request forms (mail or download) for copyright, ISBN, ABI (Advance Book Information), Library of Congress Catalog Card Number, etc. Review Chapter 5 for details and see the Appendix for sample forms.
	Visit your local library and read *Literary Market Place* for additional information.

Traditional Book Schedule Sample

Next 3 months	While Writing Your Manuscript
	Get free starter information by contacting us on our Web site www.writershelpdesk.com
	Start working on your marketing plan.
	Check Amazon.com, *Books in Print and Pending Books in Print* at the library to verify if your book title is already taken.
	Interview and select a book cover designer or design your own cover.
	Interview and select book editor/proofreader and book layout specialist (unless you will layout your own book). You can use most word processing software for your book layout. If you are familiar with PageMaker®, QuarkXPress® or other professional designer software programs, use one of those. A word of caution, this project will be extremely time consuming!
	Start requesting written testimonials, endorsements, and foreword from organizations and recognized individuals for your book. Use your book summary to mail out.

Traditional Book Schedule Sample

Final Month	When Your Manuscript is Almost Completed
	Purchase ISBN from R. R. Bowker (see Chapter 5 for details) and complete the form for processing.
	Apply for Library of Congress Catalog Card Number (see Chapter 5 for details).
	Select your book jacket or cover design that includes your testimonials, endorsements, forewords, and your photograph. Select a professional photographer for color and black & white photos.
	Interview and select a wholesaler or distributor for your book (see Chapter 9 and Appendix for listings)
	Decide on your order fulfillment method. Get an 800 number, accept credit cards, contract a fulfillment firm, etc. (see Appendix for listings)
	Secure copyright, reprint permission or any other releases for references used in your book.
	Solicit price quotes from at least 10 printers. Ask printers to provide samples of books similar to your book size. Printer quotes are usually only good for one month due to fluctuating costs.
	Determine the retail price for your book (review Chapter 3 for details).
	Prepare galleys (an unedited bound manuscript) to send for book reviews. Book reviewers will need 2-3 months before they notify you if your book will be selected. (See Chapter 7 for details).
	Design an authors' web site for your book. Secure a domain name.

Traditional Book Schedule Sample

D-Day	Your Manuscript is Completed
	Get a professional photograph for media kits/releases. Both color and black & white photographs should be selected. If you are using your photo on your cover, complete this project before your cover is designed.
	Select and assign an ISBN number for your book.
	Complete the ABI (Advance Book Information) form and select a publication date for your book. This is the date you will launch your publicity campaign for your book. The date is usually 3-4 months after the book is printed.
	Order your EAN bar code with your newly assigned ISBN number and book price. We recommend ordering the barcode on diskette to send to the printer for insertion on your book cover. The book cover designer should allow the spacing for your book code to be scanned onto the final cover.
	For library placement, you will need to order your P-CIP (Publisher's-Cataloging-in-Publication) from Quality Books (see Chapter 5 for details). The P-CIP information must be placed on the copyright page.
	Make final revision to your copyright page that includes your ISBN and Library of Congress Catalog number. Verify your copyright language is listed on your copyright page. Review Chapter 5 for details.

Traditional Book Schedule Sample

	Complete your book cover with your testimonials. Bar code, pricing, publishing firm name, contact information (phone, mailing address or web site, etc.)
	Send your manuscript to book editor for revisions. Allow a minimum of one month or longer for project completion. The editor should have determined an estimate of your project completion earlier.
	Discuss and make the corrections on your manuscript. Your editor can also make approved changes on a disk for faster processing and delivery.
	Send the revised and completed manuscript to your book layout specialist or typesetter.

Traditional Book Schedule Sample

D-Day	Your Manuscript is Completed
	If you are doing your book layout, set up edited manuscript in book format or layout using one of the suggested software packages in Chapter 9. Be sure to confirm that the software is acceptable to the printer.
	Select your book printer. Send completed book (formatted) and cover on diskettes to the printer. Also, send a camera-ready copy (laser jet printer acceptable) to the printer. Consider having your books shrink-wrapped in quantities of 10 or less. Shrink-wrap protects your books and convenient to count and deliver. Discuss additional cost with your printer. It's worth it.
	Rest!
	Your printer should return a blueline for final proofing and last minute changes. Check it very carefully especially the book jacket/cover and the EAN bar code. Last minute changes can be very expensive. If you receive a favorable or prestigious book review, it's worth including it on your cover. Return the blueline to the printer with any revisions. Allow 4-6 weeks for delivery of your books.
	Finish your marketing plan. Select a storage facility for your books, such as inside your home or mini-storage (climate control). Keeping your books in the garage will expose them to extreme weather (heat, cold, humidity, floods, etc.).

Traditional Book Schedule Sample

D-Day	While Your Book is Being Printed
	Develop and prepare media releases and other promotional materials. See Chapter 7 for details.
	Select online booksellers and links for your web site.
	Get a business phone and fax line for book orders. Set up your office space for operating a business. Buy an accounting software package for invoicing, bill paying and inventory control.
	Begin implementing first stage of your marketing plan by contacting bookstores, organizations, media, etc.
	Decide on which e-book publishers you will use to convert your manuscript to electronic formats.

Action!	Your Books Arrive
	Check your books for printer quality and total number delivered.
	Complete copyright form and mail books to US Copyright Office.
	Send an application and copies of books to distributor or wholesaler for review and acceptance. List and update them on the ABI form online.
	Continue to solicit book reviews from organizations, associations, book clubs, or prominent individuals by sending complimentary copies. Add these new reviews to your media kit and mail outs.
	Apply for book placement on Amazon.com, BN.com and other online book sellers.
	Start selling your books! The power of one!
	Use your marketing plan!
	Congratulations! You did it! The fun is just beginning.

Sample Forms

Obtain these sample forms on the Internet along with instructions.
See Chapter 5 for more information.

PLEASE FILL IN AS MUCH INFORMATION AS POSSIBLE OR APPLICABLE *RETURN ENTIRE FORM*

ADVANCE BOOK INFORMATION
R.R. BOWKER DATA COLLECTION CENTER
P.O. BOX 6000-0103, OLDSMAR, FL 34677-0103

TITLE: _____

SUBTITLE: _____

PUBLISHER (Not Printer): _____

Title Volume Number: _____   ADDRESS: _____

_____

Is this a set? Yes☐ No☐ Number of Volumes: _____   PHONE: _____ TOLL FREE: _____
FAX: _____ TELEX: _____

Is Title Orig. Paperbk? ☐YES ☐NO   E-mail, Internet, etc.: _____

Pub. Date: (MM/YY) _____ / _____   IMPRINT (if other than company name): _____

Copyright Date: (year) _____   DISTRIBUTOR (if other than publisher): _____
(If you distribute foreign books, please send us a copy of your documentation and indicate
Pages: _____ Illustrated?: ☐ YES ☐ NO   whether distribution is exclusive or non-exclusive. Currently, only exclusive distributors are included in the US portion of the BIP database.)

CONTRIBUTOR NAME (A=Author, E=Editor, I=Illustrator, P=Photographer, T=Translator):

Contributor _____   ☐A ☐E ☐I ☐P ☐T ☐Other _____
(check all that apply)

Contributor _____   ☐A ☐E ☐I ☐P ☐T ☐Other _____
(check all that apply)

Contributor _____   ☐A ☐E ☐I ☐P ☐T ☐Other _____
(check all that apply)

Contributor _____   ☐A ☐E ☐I ☐P ☐T ☐Other _____
(check all that apply)

Series Title: _____

Series Subtitle: _____ Series Volume Number: _____

Edition Info.: ☐Reprint ☐ Revised ☐ Abridged ☐Large Type ☐ Unabridged ☐ Other(specify) _____

Edition No.: ☐2nd ☐ 3rd ☐ 4th ☐ 5th ☐ 6th ☐ Other(specify) _____

Audience: (children's books require grade levels) GRADES: _____ AGES: _____

☐ Juvenile ☐ Young Adult ☐ ElHi—Reading Levels _____

☐ College ☐ Adult\General ☐Other (specify) _____

Original Title: (if previously published & changed) _____

Translated Title: _____

Current Language (if other than English): _____ Original Language (if translated): _____

Publisher Order No.: _____ LCCard No(LCCN): _____

Point Size (Large Type Bks.): _____ Book Size: _____ Book Weight: _____

For ISBN Applicants: Fill out this form for each of your titles and return with your application. When the top copy is returned to you
with your ISBN log book, assign an ISBN to each title, enter it below, and return the form(s) to the R.R. Bowker Data Collection
Center, Florida. This will allow us to list your title(s) with all information in our database.
ISBN Note: Write full 10-digit number in space below. The BIP system requires a separate ISBN for each edition and binding.

BINDING	ISBN	PRICE	*TYPE:	**CURRENCY	DISCOUNT	
Hardcover: ☐ Trade ☐ Textbk		$___.___	___	___	Short___	% Max___
Paperback: ☐ Trade ☐ Textbk		$___.___	___	___	Short___	% Max___
☐Library Binding		$___.___	___	___	Short___	% Max___
☐Mass Market		$___.___	___	___	Short___	% Max___
☐Other: _____		$___.___	___	___	Short___	% Max___
☐Other: _____		$___.___	___	___	Short___	% Max___

(OTHER refers to Tchr's. ed., Wkbk., Lab Manual, Looseleaf, etc.)   *Price type refers to invoice, retail, tentative, etc.   (Short Discount is 20% or less)
**Currency refers to US, Canadian, etc.

Type of Work: ☐ Non-Fiction ☐ Fiction ☐ Poetry ☐ Drama ☐ Essay ☐ Other _____

Subject Area: ☐ Children's (CB) ☐ Law(LB) ☐ Med(MB) ☐ Relig(RB) ☐ Sci-Tech(ST) ☐ Other _____

Description of Content: _____

Advance Book Information (ABI) Form

BISAC MAJOR SUBJECTS

The Book Industry Systems Advisory Committee (BISAC) has developed a list of **2000** subjects and subject codes to be used to describe the contents of a specific title. Below you will find a list of the **General Headings** for each of the **47 major categories**; please choose and mark the appropriate subject.

Please be advised that even if you use these headings, you should still complete the section entitles **"Description of Content"** at the bottom of the ABI form so that your book(s) can be properly classified in more detail for the *Subject Guide to Books in Print.*

Please Check Appropriate Subject(s)

☐ANTIQUES / COLLECTIBLES
☐ARCHITECTURE
☐ART
☐BIOGRAPHY / AUTOBIOGRAPHY / LETTERS
☐BUSINESS / ECONOMICS / FINANCE
☐COMPUTER TECHNOLOGY & SOFTWARE
☐COOKBOOKS & COOKERY
☐CRAFTS & HOBBIES
☐CURRENT AFFAIRS
☐DRAMA
☐EDUCATION & TEACHING
☐FAMILY / CHILD CARE / RELATIONSHIPS
☐FICTION / LITERATURE
☐FOREIGN LANGUAGE INSTRUCTION & REFERENCE
☐GAMES
☐GARDENING & HORTICULTURE
☐HEALTH & FITNESS
☐HISTORY
☐HOME IMPROVEMENT & CONSTRUCTION
☐HUMOR
☐JUVENILE FICTION
☐LANGUAGE ARTS
☐LAW
☐LITERARY CRITICISM & ESSAYS
☐MATHEMATICS
☐MEDICAL / NURSING / HOME CARE
☐MUSIC
☐NATURE & NATURAL HISTORY
☐OCCULTISM / PARAPSYCHOLOGY
☐PERFORMING ARTS
☐PETS & PET CARE
☐PHILOSOPHY
☐PHOTOGRAPHY
☐POETRY
☐POLITICAL SCIENCE & GOVERNMENT
☐PSYCHOLOGY / PSYCHIATRY
☐REFERENCE
☐RELIGION / BIBLES
☐SCIENCE
☐SELF-ACTUALIZATION / SELF-HELP
☐SOCIAL SCIENCES
☐SPORTS & RECREATION
☐STUDY AIDS
☐TECHNOLOGY & INDUSTRIAL ARTS
☐TRANSPORTATION
☐TRAVEL & TRAVEL GUIDES
☐TRUE CRIME

ABI Application- Subjects

ISBN

INTERNATIONAL STANDARD BOOK NUMBER--UNITED STATES AGENCY
International Standard Numbering System for the Information Industry
121 Chanlon Road, New Providence, New Jersey 07974
TEL: 877-310-7333 FAX: 908-665-2895 Email: isbn-san@bowker.com

International Standard ISO
2108

R.R. Bowker, A division of Reed Elsevier Inc.

APPLICATION FOR AN ISBN PUBLISHER PREFIX

FOR AGENCY USE ONLY

SYMBOL: _____

PREFIX: _____

PLEASE PRINT OR TYPE:

Company/Publisher Name: _____

Address: _____

Phone Number: _____ Fax Number: _____

Toll Free Number: _____ Telex Number: _____

E-MAIL: _____ Web Site: _____

Fax-on-Demand: _____ Toll Free Fax: _____

If P.O. Box Indicated, Local Street Address is Required:

Company Position: _____ Phone Number: _____

Name of Rights & and Permissions Contact: _____

Title: _____ Phone Number: _____

Name of ISBN Coordinator/Contact: _____

Title: _____ Phone Number: _____

Division or Subsidiary of: _____

Imprints: _____

ISBN Application

PAYMENT: A NON-REFUNDABLE PROCESSING SERVICE CHARGE
         PRIORITY PROCESSING SURCHARGE $50

ISBN PREFIX BLOCK	REGULAR PROCESSING FEE	PRIORITY PROCESSING FEE
10 ISBNs	$225.00	$275.00
100 ISBNs	$800.00	$850.00
1,000 ISBNs	$1,200.00	$1,250.00
10,000 ISBNs	$3,000.00	-

Fee Waiver:
Applicants requesting a fee-waiver MUST provide a list of titles and
formats along with 501(C3) and mission statement documents.
Failure to provide this title list will delay Agency processing.

__ Check/Money Order enclosed.   Make payable to "R. R. Bowker."

__ Charge: ____ American Express ____ Visa ____ Master Card

Card Holder Name: _____

       Account #: _____ Expiration Date: _____

Total amount enclosed or charged: _____

Authorized signature: _____ Date: _____

* Note: Credit Cards are **the preferred form of payment**

PUBLISHING INFORMATION:

1. Indicate year you started publishing: _____

2. Indicate what type of products you produce (circle):

   Books   Videos   Spoken Words on Cassette/CD
         Software   Mixed Media

   Other - Please specify: _____

3. Book Subject Area (circle):

   o Children's
   o Law
   o Medical
   o Religious
   o Sci-Tech
   o Other - Please specify: _____

DISTRIBUTION INFORMATION:

1. Do you distribute for, or are you distributed by, any other company?
   Yes: _____ No: _____. If yes, please provide full company name,
   address and ISBN Publisher Prefix (if any):

   _____
   _____
   _____

PROCESSING INFORMATION:

ISBN Application – Page 2

SHORT FORM TX

For a Nondramatic Literary Work
UNITED STATES COPYRIGHT OFFICE

Registration Number

| | TX | TXU |

Effective Date of Registration

Application Received

Deposit Received
One | Two

Fee Received

Examined By

Correspondence ☐

TYPE OR PRINT IN BLACK INK. DO NOT WRITE ABOVE THIS LINE.

1 Title of This Work:

Alternative title or title of larger work in which this work was published:

2 Name and Address of Author and Owner of the Copyright:

Nationality or domicile:
Phone, fax, and email:

Phone ( )   Fax ( )
Email

3 Year of Creation:

4 If work has been published, Date and Nation of Publication:

a. Date _____ _____ _____ *(Month, day, and year all required)*
       Month   Day   Year
b. Nation

5 Type of Authorship in This Work:

Check all that this author created.

☐ Text (includes fiction, nonfiction, poetry, computer programs, etc.)
☐ Illustrations
☐ Photographs
☐ Compilation of terms or data

6 Signature:

Registration cannot be completed without a signature.

I certify that the statements made by me in this application are correct to the best of my knowledge. Check one:
☐ Author ☐ Authorized agent

X _

7 Name and Address of Person to Contact for Rights and Permissions:
Phone, fax, and email:

☐ Check here if same as #2 above.

Phone ( )   Fax ( )
Email

8 Certificate will be mailed in window envelope to this address:

Name ▼

Number/Street/Apt ▼

City/State/ZIP ▼

9 Complete this space only if you currently hold a Deposit Account in the Copyright Office.

Deposit Account # _____
Name _____

DO NOT WRITE HERE   Page 1 of ____ pages

Copyright Application

✐ Instructions for Short Form TX ✐

For nondramatic literary works, including fiction and nonfiction, books, short stories, poems, collections of poetry, essays, articles in serials, and computer programs

USE THIS FORM IF—

1. You are the **only** author and copyright owner of this work, *and*
2. The work was **not** made for hire, *and*
3. The work is completely new (does not contain a substantial amount of material that has been previously published or registered or is in the public domain).

If any of the above does not apply, you must use standard Form TX.
NOTE: *Short Form TX is not appropriate for an anonymous author who does not wish to reveal his or her identity.*

HOW TO COMPLETE SHORT FORM TX

■ Type or print in black ink.

■ Be clear and legible. (Your certificate of registration will be copied from your form.)

■ Give only the information requested.

NOTE: You may use a continuation sheet (Form __/CON) to list individual titles in a collection. Complete Space A and list the individual titles under Space C on the back page. Space B is not applicable to short forms.

1 Title of This Work

You must give a title. If there is no title, state "UNTITLED." If you are registering an unpublished collection, give the collection title you want to appear in our records (for example: "Joan's Poems, Volume I"). Alternative title: If the work is known by two titles, you also may give the second title. If the work has been published as part of a larger work (including a periodical), give the title of that larger work in addition to the title of the contribution.

2 Name and Address of Author and Owner of the Copyright

Give your name and mailing address. You may include your pseudonym followed by "pseud." Also, give the nation of which you are a citizen or where you have your domicile (i.e., permanent residence). Please give daytime phone and fax numbers and email address, if available.

3 Year of Creation

Give the latest year in which you completed the work you are registering at this time. A work is "created" when it is written down, stored in a computer, or otherwise "fixed" in a tangible form.

4 Publication

If the work has been published (i.e., if copies have been distributed to the public), give the complete date of publication (month, day, and year) and the nation where the publication first took place.

5 Type of Authorship in This Work

Check the box or boxes that describe your authorship in the copy you are sending with the application. For example, if you are registering a story and are planning to add illustrations later, check only the box for "text."

A "compilation" of terms or of data is a selection, coordination, or arrangement of such information into a chart, directory, or other form. A compilation of previously published or public domain material must be registered using a standard Form TX.

6 Signature of Author

Sign the application in black ink and check the appropriate box. The person signing the application should be the author or his/her authorized agent.

7 Person to Contact for Rights and Permissions

This space is optional. You may give the name and address of the person or organization to contact for permission to use the work. You may also provide phone, fax, or email information.

8 Certificate Will Be Mailed

This space must be completed. Your certificate of registration will be mailed in a window envelope to this address. Also, if the Copyright Office needs to contact you, we will write to this address.

9 Deposit Account

Complete this space only if you currently maintain a deposit account in the Copyright Office.

MAIL WITH THE FORM

■ A $30 (effective through June 30, 2002) filing fee in the form of a check or money order *(no cash)* payable to "Register of Copyrights," **and**

■ One or two copies of the work. If the work is unpublished, send one copy. If published, send two copies of the best published edition. (If first published outside the U.S., send one copy either as first published or of the best edition.) **Note:** Inquire about special requirements for works first published before 1978. Copies submitted become the property of the U.S. Government.

Mail everything **(application form, copy or copies, and fee)** *in one package* to:

Library of Congress
Copyright Office
101 Independence Avenue, S.E.
Washington, D.C. 20559-6000

QUESTIONS? Call (202) 707-3000 [TTY: (202) 707-6737] between 8·30 a.m. and 5:00 p.m. eastern time, Monday through Friday. For forms and informational circulars, call (202) 707-9100 24 hours a day, 7 days a week, or download them from the Internet at www.loc.gov/copyright. Selected informational circulars but not forms are available from Fax-on-Demand at (202) 707-2600.

PRIVACY ACT ADVISORY STATEMENT Required by the Privacy Act of 1974 (P.L. 93-579)
The authority for requesting this information is title 17 U.S.C., secs. 409 and 410. Furnishing the requested information is voluntary. But if the information is not furnished, it may be necessary to delay or refuse registration and you may not be entitled to certain relief, remedies, and benefits provided in chapters 4 and 5 of title 17 U.S.C.
The principal uses of the requested information are the establishment and maintenance of a public record and the examination of the application for compliance with the registration requirements of the copyright law.
Other routine uses include public inspection and copying, preparation of public indexes, preparation of public catalogs of copyright registrations, and preparation of search reports upon request.
NOTE: No other advisory statement will be given in connection with this application. Please keep this statement and refer to it if we communicate with you regarding this application.

Copyright Form Instruction Sheet

REQUEST FOR PREASSIGNMENT OF LIBRARY OF CONGRESS CATALOG CARD NUMBER

NOTE: *Card numbers cannot be preassigned to books which are already published. Works that receive a preassigned Library of Congress catalog card number are not eligible to receive Cataloging in Publication data for that same edition of the work.*

FORM MUST BE TYPED   DATE: _____

PUBLISHER'S NAME ON TITLE PAGE: _____

YOUR NAME: _____   PHONE NUMBER: _____

Type the complete address to which the preassigned card number should be sent. (This will be your return mailing label.)

```
 ┌                          ┐      ┌──────────────────────────────┐
                                   │   FOR CIP OFFICE USE          │
                                   │                              │
                                   │   Library of Congress Catalog │
                                   │   Card Number preassigned is: │
 └                          ┘      └──────────────────────────────┘
```

Transcribe the information in items 1-8 exactly in the form and order in which it will appear on the title or copyright pages of the printed book. Use only those abbreviations which will actually appear on these pages. **(Please attach a copy of the proposed title page, if available.)**

1. Author(s) _____

2. Editor(s) _____

3. Title _____

4. Subtitle _____

5. Edition (exactly as printed in the publication, e.g. second edition, revised edition, etc.) _____

6. U.S. place of publication: City _____ State _____

7. Any copublisher(s) and place _____

8. Series title and numbering, exactly as printed in the publication _____

9. Approximate number of pages _____ 10. Number of volumes _____

11. ISBN (Hard cover) _____ ISBN (Paperback) _____

12. Proposed date of publication: Month _____ Year _____ 13. Language of text, if other than English _____

14. Does (or will) the title in item 3 appear at periodic intervals, e.g. annually, quarterly, etc.? ☐ Yes ☐ No

For each title which is preassigned a Library of Congress catalog card number, the Library of Congress requires one non-returnable complimentary copy of the best edition of the published book. If selected for the Library's collections, the book will be cataloged. This copy is in addition to copyright deposit copies. Continuing participation in the PCN program is contingent on full compliance with this obligation.

Send this form to: Library of Congress
Cataloging in Publication Division
101 Independence Ave., S.E.
Washington, DC 20540-4320

LCCN Application

Glossary of Common Publishing Terms

AAP: Association of American Publishers.

ABA: American Booksellers Association. This trade association of non-chain bookstores hosts a huge international annual book convention the week after the Memorial Day weekend.

ABI: Advanced Book Information. This form is completed to have your book listed in *Books in Print* and *Forthcoming Books in Print.*

Account Receivable: Money owed to a business by customers who have been granted credit by the business.

Acid Free Paper: Book printing paper made without acid to help extend the life or appearance of the paper.

Acquisitions Editor: The contact person in a publishing house who gathers new manuscripts.

Advance: Money paid to an author upon signing a publishing contract. Once the publisher recovers this amount from book sales, the author usually begins to receive book royalties.

Afterword: Final comments from the author. The afterword usually follows the last chapter of the book.

ALA: American Library Association.

Artwork: Images used in producing a book or other work other than straight text.

Author: A writer who has completed a book.

Anthology: A collection of written material by one of more authors published as a single literary work.

Back List: Books still in print but not considered new.

Back Order: An order that is not currently in stock but scheduled to be filled when available.

Bar Code: The coding system found on the back cover that identifies books and automates pricing, ordering and tracking book inventories. Books use the Bookland EAN bar code system.

Belt Press: A printing press that can print multiple pages at one time.

Best Seller: A top-selling book. There are several best-selling lists.

Bibliography: A listing of reference material used by the author in the preparation of a book or suggested by the author for his or her readers.

Bill of Lading: Papers shipped with an order that itemizes the contents of the package. Also may be called *packing slip.*

Bio: A brief statement about an author's background, accomplishments, qualifications, and/or interests. For example, a bio is included in a media kit.

Bleed: Images or ink printed all the way to the edge of the book cover.

Blueline: A proof sheet made from a negative and produced in blue ink that shows how the book will look when printed. A printer will provide you a blueline of your entire book for final proofing before the book is bound and printed.

Blurbs: Positive but brief comments about a book usually for promotional purposes.

Bold: Type that is heavier and darker than regular or standard text type. Also may be called *boldface.*

Book: A publication consisting of 49 or more pages that is bound and not a periodical or serial.

Book Broker: A person or company that finds book printers for authors or publishers and adds in their fee for this service.

Booklet: A small book or publication consisting of less than 49 pages. A booklet usually has a softcover

Bookland EAN: The type of bar code system used in the book industry. Bookland EAN/5 is a common book bar code.

Book Packager: An entrepreneur who creates clever ways to produce books, hires writers to assist, and then sells the completed work to a publisher. A creative book packager can help create new markets for a book.

Camera Ready: Camera ready is the final text and graphics of a book that is ready to be copied, photographed, or otherwise reproduced by a printer of your book.

Cataloging-in-Publication: Information listed on the copyright page of a book that is provided by the Library of Congress to help libraries shelve a book in the correct category.

Chapbook: A small book of poems, ballads, or tales.

CIP: Cataloging in Publication.

Clip Art: General use graphics that can be clipped, downloaded or otherwise used as an illustration in a book or other print.

Clipping Service: A service company that looks at newspaper, magazines, and other articles across the country of interest to another company or person and clips them out for a fee.

Collating: Compiling printed sheets of paper in a set format or order.

Coated Paper: Paper that is processed or coated to be shiny or extra smooth.

Comb Binding: Spiral-shaped plastic binding that is used to bind a book together. This type of binding is often used in journals, workbooks, or cookbooks.

Co-Op Advertising: Sharing the costs of advertising for a common goal.

Co-publishing: Two or more parties accepting different duties and/or financial commitments to publish one book.

Copy Editing: Technical reviews of a manuscript for correct spelling, grammar, etc.

Copyright: Copyright is the legal right given to protect an individual or company from others copying written, graphic or other works they have created.

Copyright Notice: The notice printed on the copyright page of a book that creates additional legal protection for the copyright owner. Example: © 1999 John Doe.

Copyright Year: The year stated in the copyright notice.

Cover Letter: A brief letter sent along with a manuscript.

Crop Marks: The lines or other marks or symbols used to instruct the printer where the text will be printed in a book.

DBA: *Doing Business As*. A fictitious name used by a sole proprietorship or other business form instead of their actual name. Example: John Doe DBA *Doe Publishing*.

DVD: Digital Video Disk

Direct Mail: Advertising material mailed directly to a targeted buyer.

Display Ad: A type of advertisement that usually uses both text and graphics to sell a product or service in a magazine, newspaper, or other print.

Distributor: When referring to the book trade, a company that warehouses books of publishers and then markets or sells them to bookstores, retail stores, libraries, etc. They usually have a sales force that actively visits established clients or stores that may buy your book.

Domain Name: The text name relating to the numeric Internet provider or IP address of a server or computer on the Internet (e.g., writershelpdesk.com is a domain name.)

Drop Ship: Shipping an order directly from the manufacturer to a designated address that is different from the person or company that is actually paying for the product.

Dump: Types of displays used to market or house a book or other product in a store.

Dust Jacket: The graphic paper cover of a hardbound book.

E-books: Electronic or digital books. Books printed in electronic format instead of on paper.

E-commerce: Electronic commerce. This provides the ability to accept credit card and other payment methods on a web site to effect purchases of goods and services.

Editing: Changing or correcting the contents of a book to improve its quality.

Edition: The unaltered or original printing of a book. The edition number changes when a change is made to the content of the book. Example: Our first edition of a book was expanded from 108 pages to 230 pages. The new book is now the second edition.

Epilogue: Text at the end of a book that updates the reader about the book or author.

Exclusive rights: Rights given to only one party to perform a service. Once given no one can perform the service for a specified period. Book distributors usually want exclusive rights to market and distribute a book to chain bookstores or their specific retail market.

Fiction: Novels and other writings that are stories created or imagined by the author.

Film Lamination: A thin plastic coat placed on a book cover for protective purposes.

First Edition: The original or first print run of a book.

FOB: Free On Board. Example: FOB Houston means the item are free as far as Houston; the buyer pays the shipping beyond Houston.

Font: A complete set of type in a unique style. Examples of types of font are Times New Roman, Arial, and Courier New.

Foreword: Remarks made in the front of the book before the introduction that praise the author. Usually someone well known or influential on the subject of the book writes the foreword.

Front Matter: The pages in the front of a book *before* the main text or chapters.

Fulfillment Company: A company that handles ordering, credit card processing, packing, and shipping of a product for a fee.

Galley: A sample version of a book without the final cover before it goes to print. Book reviewers that want to see the book several months before it is printed often require a galley.

Genre: A category type of a book. Example: inspirational, sci-fi.

Ghostwriter: A professional that writes books for other persons.

Halftone: A process that reproduces a black and white photograph using tiny dots to make it easier to print in a book.

Hard Cover: A more expensive way to bind a book with a hardbound cover versus a less expensive paperback cover.

Headshot: A photograph of an author used for publicity purposes.

Imprint: The name a publishing company uses on the title page. Some companies may have several imprints or division names.

In Print: Books that are still available for sale.

ISBN: International Standard Book Number. A unique number that identifies each edition of a book that's similar to your social security number. It's a ten-digit number (sometimes alpha/numeric).

Internet: A network of computers linked together that communicates in a common language.

Jacket: The paper cover of a hard cover book.

Jobber: A type of distributor that buys large quantities of books that are sold on bookracks in retail stores.

Layout: Putting the pages of a book together in the form in which it will appear when it printed.

Library of Congress: The library of the U.S. Congress located in Washington, D.C.

Library of Congress Catalog Card Number: A unique number obtained from the Library of Congress to help libraries identify books. This number is a minimum requirement for publishers who want to sell their books to libraries.

Literary Entrepreneur: A self-published author or small press.

LMP: *Literary Market Place.* The book publishing industry's premier directory for references.

Mail Order: Filling an order by delivering the product through the mail.

Manuscript: A book in typed or handwritten form before it is typeset for a printer. Most printers prefer to have manuscripts sent on disks, but they will accept camera-ready printed copies.

Marketing Plan: The road map or guide to successfully market or sell a book to the people or businesses an author or publisher wants to buy the book. A marketing plan may be part of a comprehensive business plan.

Matte: A dull surface.

Media Kit: A package of promotional material created for the media and used to bring attention to a book or event.

Newsgroup: A group of individuals communicating through the Internet on a subject of mutual interest.

News Release: An announcement sent to a newspaper, radio station, television station, or other media to promote a product, event, or service. Also called a *press release.*

Non-Fiction: Writings based on fact.

Out of Print: A book no longer available from the publisher for sale.

Overrun: Print runs exceeding the actual amount of books ordered.

POD: Print on demand. This is printing small quantities of books upon request within 48 hours using digital technology.

Packing Slip: Papers shipped with an order that itemizes the contents of the package. Also may be called *bill of lading.*

Paperback: A soft-cover book.

Pagination: The process by which pages of a book are numbered or set in a certain order.

Pen name: Fictitious name used by an author. Also may be called a pseudonym.

Perfect Binding: The standard binding commonly required by bookstores where the cover is glued on and has a flat spine where the name of the book and author is printed.

Permissions: Approval to use material of others that is protected by copyrights.

Preface: Remarks made by the author in the front matter of a book to explain the purpose of the book.

Pre-Publication: Before publication.

Press Kit: A package of promotional material created for the media and used to bring attention to a book or event.

Press Release: An announcement sent to newspaper, radio station, television station, or other media to promote a product, event, or service. Also called *news release,* the preferred term.

Proposal: An idea for a book.

PMA: Publishers Marketing Association. This trade association provides a number of services designed to help its members sell books.

PSA: Public Service Announcement.

Public Domain: Material not protected by a copyright.

Publication Date: The date for which a book's major publicity is scheduled and books are available for sale.

Publicist: A person who plans the publicity campaign of an author.

Public Relations Firm: A firm that plans promotions and publicity for a company or individual.

Publisher: A person or company that handles all the activities necessary to produce a book.

Query Letter: A letter written to a publisher by an author or agent to stimulate interest in a book project.

Reprint: An additional printing of a book.

Returns: Books that are returned back to the publisher because they are not selling or are damaged.

Review: An evaluation of a book by a newspaper, magazine, person, or other source.

Review Copy: A free copy of a book given to a source in a position to write a review.

RFQ: Request for quotation.

Royalty: A pre-determined percentage paid to an author by the publisher for books sold.

Saddle Stitch: The type of binding that uses staples. This is typically used in magazines, booklets, and brochures.

Sales Rep: A person who sells books for several different publishers for a commission.

Sheet-Fed Press: A press that prints a single sheet or page at a time.

Short Run: A small printing of books.

Soft Cover: Paperback cover.

Spam: Unsolicited or junk e-mail.

Spine: The section of the book that binds the front cover to the back cover.

Spiral Binding: Spiral wire binding used to bind books, journals, notebooks, etc.

SAN: Standard Address Number. A SAN is a unique seven-digit identifying number used to indicate a specific address of a company directly or indirectly related to the publishing industry.

Subsidiary Rights: Additional rights to publish a book but in a different manner. Such rights include foreign rights, book clubs rights, and serial rights.

Subsidy Press: Often used to mean the same as a vanity press.

Target Audience: The people or organizations you want to buy your book.

Tear Sheets: Ads torn from an upcoming magazine as proof of their printing.

Text: The main body of a book.

URL: Uniform Resource Locator. A method by which a browser locates an exact location on the Internet. For example, www.urgems.com is a URL.

Vanity Press: A non-traditional publisher who charges the author to publish his or her book.

Velo-Bind: A form of binding that punches holes into the paper and attaches two strips of plastic to hold the pages together.

Web Press: A printing press that uses large rolls of papers instead of single sheets to print books.

Web site: A page or pages on the Internet or World Wide Web.

Wholesaler: A company that buys from publishers and fills orders from bookstores, libraries, etc. They are different from distributors because they do not normally have a sales staff. Also, they do not normally care if you use more than one wholesaler.

With the Grain: Printing in the same direction as the grain of the paper.

Bibliography/Recommended Reading

Abraham, Jay. *Getting Everything You Can Out Of All You've Got,* New York, New York: Truman Talley Books, 2000.

Adair-Hoy, Angela. *How to Publish A Profitable E-mag,* Andover, MA: Deep South Publishing Company, 1999.
Bard, Mitchell G. "Electronic books". *Writers Digest,* December 1999.

Canfield, Jack, Mark Victor Hansen, and Bud Gardner. *Chicken Soup for the Writer's Soul,* Deerfield Beach, FL: Health Communications, Inc., 2000.

Fleming, Robert. *The African American Writer's Handbook.* New York, New York: One World, 2000.

Jassin, Lloyd J. and Steven C. Schechter. *The Copyright Permission and Libel Handbook.* New York, New York: John Wiley & Sons, Inc., 1998.

Jenkins, Jerrold R. and Stanton, Anne M. *Publish To Win.* Traverse City, Michigan: Rhodes & Easton, 1997.

Jud, Brian. *Perpetual Promotion.* Avon, CT: Marketing Directions, Inc., 1997.

Kavka, Dorothy & Heise, Dan. *The Successful Self-Publisher.* Evanston, Illinois: Evanston Publishing, Inc., 1996.

King, Stephen. *A Memoir of the Craft on Writing.* New York, NY: Scribner. 2000

Kremer, John. *1001 Ways to Market Your Book,* 5th Edition. Fairfield, Iowa: Open Horizons, 2000.*

Kremer, John. "Making Sense of Your E-book Options – Part II." *Book Marketing Update*, January 30, 2000, pp. 1-5.

Poynter, Dan. *The Self-Publishing Manual,* 12th Edition. Santa Barbara, California : Para Publishing, 2000.*

Ross, Tom & Marilyn. *Jump Start Your Book Sales.* Buena Vista, Colorado: Communication Creativity, 1999.

Rubie, Peter. *The Everything Get Published Book* Holbrook, Massachusetts: Adams Media, 2000.

Smith, Sara Freeman. *Turning Stones Into Gems*: Houston, Texas: U R Gems Group, Inc., 1998.*

Strunk, William E., Jr. and White, E. B. *The Elements of Style:* Needham Heights, MA, Allyn & Bacon, 2000.

Sugihara, Kenzi and Eugene G. Schwartz. "The New Digital Demand Publishing Industry: Sorting out 21st Century Strategies for Independent Publishers." *PMA Newsletter*, August 1999, pp. 18-21.

The Chicago Manual of Style, 14th Edition: Chicago IL, University of Chicago Press, 1993.

Tedder, Lorna. *Book Promotion For The Shameless.* Niceville, FL: Spilled Candy Books, 1999.

*These are highly recommended books. *The Self-Publishing Manual* costs about $19.95 and covers virtually all facets of self-publishing. *1001 Ways to Market Your Book* costs about $29.95 and is perhaps the most comprehensive marketing resource for self-publishers. *Turning Stones Into Gems* is a motivational resource and retails for $9.95. The others are good reading material that you can check out from your local library.

Index

Order Information

☐*How to Self-Publish and Market Your Own Book* $15.95

☐*How to Self-Publish and Market Your Own Book (Workbook)* $19.95

☐*Turning Stones Into Gems* by Sara Freeman Smith $ 9.95

☐*Turning Stones Into Gems Gratitude & Prayer Journal* $ 9.95

☐Send information on available workshops.

Please Print

Name:_____

Address:_____

City:_____St_____Zip_____

Phone: (   )_____Fax (   )_____

E-mail:_____

Please add $3.00 S/H and $1.00 for each additional item ordered.
Texas residents add 8.25% sales tax.

Please check one:

☐ Check   ☐Visa   ☐Money Order
☐ American Express   ☐Master Card

Credit Card #_____Exp. Date_____

Signature_____
(as it appears on the credit card)

U R Gems Group, P. O. Box 440341, Houston, TX 77244-0341
(281) 596-8330   (281) 596-0028 Fax
Outside Houston (800) 500-2570
E-mail: urgems@aol.com
Web site: www.urgems.com

About The Authors

Mack E. Smith is Executive Vice President and Chief Operating Officer of U R Gems Group. He is fond of saying: "I did not choose publishing, publishing chose me". His wife, Sara Freeman Smith, a motivational speaker and trainer, was inspired in 1997 to write her first book, *Turning Stones Into Gems,* an inspirational, self-development system. Having acquired years of experience in finance and marketing in the business world, he offered to lend a hand with some of the details. U R Gems Group was then formed.

The success of Sara's books lead to many inquiries from other aspiring writers. Consequently, the company started a series of career development seminars for aspiring writers and motivational speakers. *How To Self-Publish & Market Your Own Book* was later published to further assist writers and meet the demand for this information.

Sara is President and Chief Executive Officer of U R Gems Group. She can inform while at the same time inspire. Sara has been speaking since 1989 on a variety of topics to diverse audiences. She has more than 20 years of executive management experience. Sara has assisted and placed thousands of individuals in various positions within small to Fortune 500 size companies.

The primary focus of U R Gems Group is motivational and career development training through workshops and personal coaching. Mack and Sara reside in Houston, Texas and have teenage son, Rashod.

The authors are available for workshops, consultation, and speaking engagements. Contact U R Gems Group at 281-596-8330 for more details.

SPECIAL OFFER

The publishing industry is rapidly growing and changing. This presents special challenges for self-publishers to keep current with industry events and issues. Like small businesses or entrepreneurs, self-publishers must wear many hats in order to be successful. To provide a venue for authors and small publishers to network, find resources, and remain current with technological changes affecting the publishing industry, we have created the Literary Entrepreneur Network.

The first 1,000 individuals signing up on the mailing list of Literary Entrepreneur Network will receive a free six-month membership. To qualify for the free membership, simply send your name, address, telephone number, and reference code:HTSP06-01 to our e-mail address, sales@literaryentrepreneur.com. You may also sign up on the web sites www.urgems.com and www.writershelpdesk.com.

Some of the benefits you will enjoy by joining the network are:
- Free publishing and marketing teleclasses
- Forums on subjects of interest to self-published authors
- Discounts on annual conference
- One hour of free telephone personal coaching
- A free e-zine
- Networking opportunities with other authors
- Access to publishing resources and information
- Discounts on workshops
- Discounts on web site development

**Our offer to a friend or family member
Give a gift to help fulfill their dream....**

Gift Order Information

☐*How to Self-Publish and Market Your Own Book* $15.95

☐*How to Self-Publish and Market Your Own Book (Workbook)* $19.95

☐*Turning Stones Into Gems* by Sara Freeman Smith $ 9.95

☐*Turning Stones Into Gems Gratitude & Prayer Journal* $ 9.95

☐Send information on available workshops.

Please Print

Name:_____

Address:_____

City:_____St_____Zip_____

Phone: (   )_____Fax (   )_____

E-mail:_____

Please add $3.00 S/H and $1.00 for each additional item ordered.
Texas residents add 8.25% sales tax.

Please check one:

☐ Check   ☐Visa   ☐Money Order
☐ American Express   ☐Master Card

Credit Card #_____Exp. Date_____

Signature_____
(as it appears on the credit card)

**U R Gems Group, P. O. Box 440341, Houston, TX 77244-0341
(281) 596-8330   (281) 596-0028 Fax
Outside Houston (800) 500-2570
E-mail: urgems@aol.com
Web site: www.urgems.com**

If you can see it,

You can believe it,

Then you can achieve it!

Our offer to a friend or family member
Give a gift to help fulfill their dream....

Gift Order Information

☐*How to Self-Publish and Market Your Own Book* $15.95

☐*How to Self-Publish and Market Your Own Book (Workbook)* $19.95

☐*Turning Stones Into Gems* by Sara Freeman Smith $ 9.95

☐*Turning Stones Into Gems Gratitude & Prayer Journal* $ 9.95

☐Send information on available workshops.

Please Print

Name:_____

Address:_____

City:_____St_____Zip_____

Phone: (   )_____Fax (   )_____

E-mail:_____

Please add $3.00 S/H and $1.00 for each additional item ordered.
Texas residents add 8.25% sales tax.

Please check one:

☐ Check   ☐Visa   ☐Money Order
☐ American Express   ☐Master Card

Credit Card #_____Exp. Date_____

Signature_____
(as it appears on the credit card)

**U R Gems Group, P. O. Box 440341, Houston, TX 77244-0341
(281) 596-8330 ◆ (281) 596-0028 Fax
Outside Houston (800) 500-2570
E-mail: urgems@aol.com
Web site: www.urgems.com**